中英文版高速铁路运营管理系列教材
Chinese-English High Speed Railway Operation Management Coursebook Series

U1007020

高速铁路车站与线路

HIGH SPEED RAILWAY STATIONS AND LINES

主　编　李云飞　徐　昕
副主编　李精忠　杨图南　赵力耀　张世涛
　　　　刘铭智　尤海波　王　杰
翻　译　张晓清　杨　钊

云南出版集团
云南人民出版社

图书在版编目（CIP）数据

高速铁路车站与线路 / 李云飞, 徐昕主编 ; 张晓清, 杨钊翻译. -- 昆明 : 云南人民出版社, 2021.12
中英文版高速铁路运营管理系列教材
ISBN 978-7-222-20156-9

Ⅰ. ①高… Ⅱ. ①李… ②徐… ③张… ④杨… Ⅲ. ①高速铁路—铁路线路—高等职业教育—教材—汉、英②高速铁路—铁路车站—高等职业教育—教材—汉、英 Ⅳ. ①U238

中国版本图书馆CIP数据核字(2021)第206852号

出 品 人： 赵石定
责任编辑： 冯　琰
助理编辑： 谢筑娟
责任校对： 胡元青
封面设计： 张益珲
责任印制： 马文杰

高速铁路车站与线路

GAOSU TIELU CHEZHAN YU XIANLU

主　编： 李云飞　徐　昕
副主编： 李精忠　杨图南　赵力耀　张世涛
刘铭智　尤海波　王　杰
翻　译： 张晓清　杨　钊

出　版　云南出版集团　云南人民出版社
发　行　云南人民出版社
社　址　昆明市环城西路609号
邮　编　650034
网　址　www.ynpph.com.cn
E-mail　ynrms@sina.com
开　本　787mm×1092mm　1/16
印　张　13.25
字　数　261千
版　次　2021年12月第1版第1次印刷
印　刷　云南金伦云印实业股份有限公司
书　号　ISBN 978-7-222-20156-9
定　价　45.00元

云南人民出版社微信公众号

如需购买图书、反馈意见，请与我社联系

总编室：0871-64109126　发行部：0871-64108507　审校部：0871-64164626　印制部：0871-64191534

前　言

Preface

《高速铁路车站与线路》采用中英文对照排版模式，为中外读者深入解读高速铁路车站与线路的相关知识。教材比较全面、系统地阐述了高速铁路车站和线路的基本知识、基本概念、基本原理、相关标准规范等内容。教材本着促进职业教育科学化、标准化、规范化的原则，运用创新的教学方法，设置了项目、任务、模块等教学单元，具有非常强的操作性、指导性和实用性，侧重对行业标准规范内容的执行和应用。教材每个任务包括学前准备、课堂学习、课堂练习、课后拓展4个模块，学中做、做中学，可充分调动教师教学能动性，丰富课堂教学内容与形式，激发学生的主动性与学习兴趣。

本教材包括以下主要内容：高速铁路选线与主要技术标准，高速铁路线路平面及纵断面设计，高速铁路线路及道岔，高速铁路车站分布及车站设计，高速铁路客运设备及段、所布置以及高速铁路引入大城市铁路枢纽设计。

本教材针对高速铁路的车站、线路的特点和要求进行撰写，使学生在学完

High Speed Railway Stations and Lines is an English-Chinese typesetting coursebook for domestic and overseas readers to deeply understand the relevant knowledge about high speed railway stations and lines. The coursebook comprehensively and systematically expounds the basic knowledge, concepts, principles, relevant standards and specifications of high speed railway stations and lines. Based on the principle of promoting scientific, standardized and normalized vocational education, innovative teaching methods are used to set up teaching units of projects, tasks and modules, which are highly operable, instructive and practical, focusing on the implementation and application of industry standards and specifications. Each task in the coursebook includes four modules of Preparation before Class, In-class Learning, In-class Exercises and After-class Activity. The mode of practice during learning and learning through practice will highly motivate teachers, enrich teaching content and forms, and greatly inspire students.

The coursebook includes the following content: route selection and main technical standards for high speed railway, plane and profile design for high speed railway, line and turnout of high speed railway, distribution and

本课程后对高速铁路车站、线路的设计原则、特点、内容、布置方式以及主要技术标准和参数等内容有一个比较全面、系统的了解。在此基础上，由教师带领主动开展实训及现场学习，深入理解行业标准规范的内容，提升综合素质。

本教材由云南交通职业技术学院李云飞、徐昕主编并统稿，负责编写的老师有李精忠、杨图南、赵力耀、张世涛、刘铭智、尤海波、王杰，张晓清、杨钊老师负责英文部分翻译工作。

在本教材编写过程中，参考了许多同行、专家的研究成果和图书资料，在此向各位专家、作者表示诚挚的谢意。由于编者水平有限，书中难免有疏漏之处，望广大读者不吝指出，以期进一步完善。

编 者

2021 年 8 月

design of high speed railway station, passenger transport equipment and setting of depot and workshop for high speed railway, design for introducing high speed railway into railway terminal in metropolis.

This coursebook is written according to the characteristics and requirements of high speed railway stations and lines. On learning the course, students shall have a comprehensive and systematic understanding of the design principles, characteristics, contents, layout methods, main technical standards and parameters of high speed railway stations and lines. On this basis, under the guidance of teachers, students can actively carry out practical training and on-site learning, deeply understand the contents of industry standards and norms and improve their comprehensive quality.

The coursebook is chiefly compiled and edited by Li Yunfei and Xu Xin of Yunnan Jiaotong College, Li Jingzhong, Yang Tu'nan, Zhao Liyao, Zhang Shitao, Liu Mingzhi, You Haibo, Wang Jie take part in the compilation of the coursebook, and Zhang Xiaoqing, Yang Zhao are responsible for the English translation.

In the process of compilation, research and documents of many experts are also referred to, and we express sincere thanks to the experts and authors. Due to the limited knowledge of the editors, there may be omissions in the book, we expect valuable suggestions from readers for further improvement.

Editor

August 2021

目　录

项目一　绪论

Project 1　Introduction

项目二　高速铁路选线与主要技术标准

Project 2　Route Selection and Main Technical Standards for High Speed Railway

项目三　高速铁路线路平面及纵断面设计

Project 3　Plane and Profile Design for High Speed Railway

项目四　高速铁路线路及道岔

Project 4　Line and Turnout of High Speed Railway

项目五　高速铁路车站分布及车站设计

Project 5　Distribution and Design of High Speed Railway Station

项目六　高速铁路客运设备及段、所布置

Project 6　Passenger Transport Equipment and Setting of Depot and Workshop for High Speed Railway

项目七　高速铁路引入大城市铁路枢纽设计

Project 7　Design for Introducing High Speed Railway into Railway Terminal in Metropolis

项目一　绪论

Project 1　Introduction

任务一　发展高速铁路的必要性

Task 1　Necessity of Developing High Speed Railway

模块一　学前准备

查一查高速铁路发展的历史：世界上最早的高速铁路在哪里，我国的第一条高速铁路是从哪里到哪里。

Module 1　Preparation before Class

Search the history of high speed railway development and find out the world's earliest high speed railway. Find out China's first high speed railway，including its starting point and ending point.

课前学习笔记
Study Notes before Class

模块二　课堂学习

知识点一：高速铁路的定义、优点和不足

1. 什么是高速铁路

高速铁路简称“高铁”，是指基础设施设计速度标准高，可供火车在轨道上安全、高速行驶的铁路，列车运营速度在 200 千米 / 时以上。高铁在不同国家、不同时代以及不同的科研学术领域有不同的定义。国家发改委将中国高铁定义为时速 200 千米及以上标准的新线或既有线路，并颁布了相应的《中长期铁路网规划》文件，将所有时速 200 千米的轨道线路统一纳入中国高速铁路网范畴。

Module 2　In-class Learning

Key Point 1：Definition，Advantages and Disadvantages of High Speed Railway

1. What is High Speed Railway

High speed railway refers to the railway with high design speed standard of infrastructure and can be used for safe and high speed running by trains on the track. The running speed of trains is above 200 km/h. High speed railway has different regulations in different countries，times and scientific research and academic fields. China's National Development and Reform Commission has defined China's high speed railway as newly-built or existing railways with a speed of 200 km/h or above，and issued the relevant document “Medium- and Long-Term Planning for China's Railway Network”，all railway lines with speed of 200 km/h are included into the category of China's high speed railway network.

高速列车最高运行速度

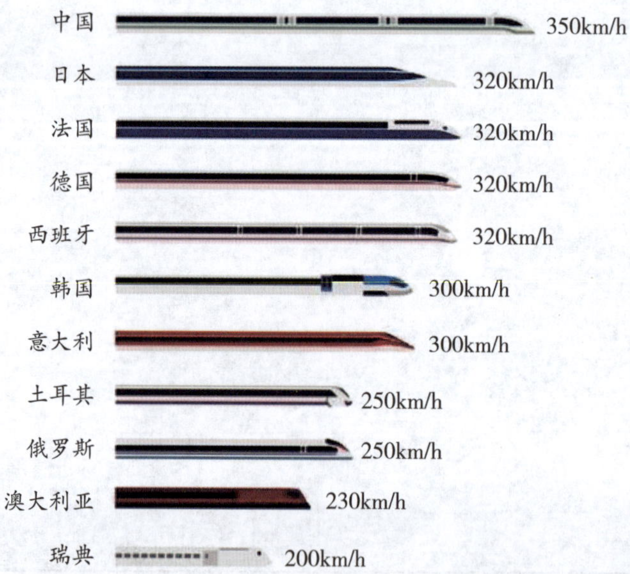

高速列车最高运行速度 maximum running speed of high speed train

中国 China　日本 Japan　法国 France　德国 Germany　西班牙 Spain　韩国 Korea　意大利 Italy

土耳其 Turkey　俄罗斯 Russia　澳大利亚 Australia　瑞典 Sweden

图 1-1　各国高铁最高时速和运营时速

Figure 1-1　Top Speed and Operating Speed of High Speed Railways in Different Countries

全世界速度最快的十大高铁，中国高铁运营时速列居第一。

2. 高速铁路的优点与不足

高速铁路的优点：速度快、耗时少、载客量大、安全性好、正点率高、舒适方便、耗能相对较低、污染小。

高速铁路的不足：投资大、运营成本高、技术要求高。

知识点二：我国发展高速铁路的必要性和规划

1. 我国发展高速铁路的必要性

（1）中国正处于经济、社会持续快速发展的重要时期，铁路“瓶颈”问题非常突出。

（2）中国正处于工业化加快形成的重要时期，铁路运输远远不能适应工业化发展的迫切要求。

（3）中国正处在统筹城乡和区域发展的关键时期，铁路网布局难以适应城乡和区域发展的迫切要求。

（4）中国正处在可持续发展的关键阶段，铁路发展未能适应综合交通运输

Among the top ten fastest high speed railways, China's high speed railway ranks first in the world.

2. Advantages and Disadvantages of High Speed Railway

Advantages: high speed, less time consumption, high passenger carrying capacity, good safety, high punctuality rate, comfort and convenience, relatively low energy consumption and less pollution.

Disadvantages: large investment, high operating cost and high technical requirements.

Key Point 2: Necessity and Planning of China's High Speed Railway Development

1. Necessity of China's High Speed Railway Development

(1) China is in an important period of sustained and rapid economic and social development, and the "bottleneck" problems in railway are obvious.

(2) China is in an important period of accelerated industrialization. Railway transportation cannot meet urgent requirements of industrial development.

(3) China is in a critical period of balancing urban-rural and regional development. The railway network cannot

体系建设的迫切要求。

meet urgent requirements of urban-rural and regional development.

（4）China is in a critical period of sustainable development. The railway development cannot meet urgent requirements of comprehensive transportation system construction.

2. 我国高速铁路的规划

“八纵八横”是国家中长期高速铁路网规划。“八纵”通道包括沿海通道、京沪通道、京港（台）通道、京哈—京港澳通道、呼南通道、京昆通道、包（银）海通道、兰（西）广通道。“八横”通道包括绥满通道、京兰通道、青银通道、陆桥通道、沿江通道、沪昆通道、厦渝通道、广昆通道。

2. China's High Speed Railway Planning

The “Eight Vertical and Eight Horizontal” is the medium and long-term high speed railway network plan as made by the state. To be specific，the “Eight Vertical” passages include the coastal passage, Beijing-Shanghai passage，Beijing-Hong Kong（Taiwan）passage，Beijing-Harbin~Beijing-Hong Kong-Macao passage, Hohhot-Nantong passage，Beijing-Kunming passage，Baotou（Yinchuan）-Haikou passage，and Lanzhou（Xi'an）-Guangzhou passage. The “Eight Horizontal” passages include Suifenhe-Manzhouli passage, Beijing-Lanzhou passage，Qingdao-Yinchuan passage，land bridge passage，Yangtze Riverside passage，Shanghai-Kunming passage，Xiamen-Chongqing passage and Guangzhou-Kunming passage.

学习笔记

Study Notes

模块三 课堂练习

问题1：查查各国高铁的时速规定。

问题2：查查我国高铁的“八横八纵”，在图上画出来。

Module 3 In-class Exercises

Question 1: Find out the speed definition of high speed railway in various countries.

Question 2: Find out the “Eight Horizontal and Eight Vertical” high speed railway network in China and draw it on the map.

课堂练习

In-class Exercises

模块四　课后拓展

收集资料，说明发展高速铁路的必要性。

Module 4　After-class Activity

Collect data to illustrate the necessity of developing high speed railway.

课后拓展

After-class Activity

任务二　高速铁路线路修建的模式

Task 2　Construction Mode of High Speed Railway Line

模块一　学前准备

查查你所在的地方有没有高铁，是怎么修建的。

Module 1　Preparation before Class

Find out if there is a high speed railway in the place where you live. If yes，how it was built.

课前学习笔记

Study Notes before Class

模块二　课堂学习

知识点：高速铁路线路修建的主要模式及特点

1. 改造既有线模式

（1）定义。

既有线指原先已经建造好的线路。通常，要对某线路进行改造时，称之为既有线。

（2）优缺点。

优点：工程量小，对城市规划的影响小。

缺点：运营存在困难，速度和通过能力受限制。

（3）适用条件。

既有条件良好，用量不是太大的情况。

2. 自成系统，新建高铁客运专线

（1）定义。

修建新线，自成系统，高速开行。

（2）优缺点。

优点：运营自成系统，速度和通过能力得到充分发挥。

缺点：工程量大，与城市中心存在衔接是否便利的问题。

（3）适用条件。

客运量大的特大城市之间。

Module 2　In-class Learning

Key Point: Main Construction Mode and Feature of High Speed Railway Line

1. Reconstruction of Existing Railway Mode

（1）Definition.

Existing railways are the originally built lines, usually when they are to be reconstructed.

（2）Advantages and disadvantages.

Advantages: small quantities of work and less impact on city overall planning.

Disadvantages: operational difficulties, limited speed and carrying capacity.

（3）Applicable condition.

Existing conditions are good, and usage amount is not too large.

2. Develop Its Own System and Build New High Speed Passenger Dedicated Lines

（1）Definition.

Construct a new line, and develop its own system with high speed operation.

（2）Advantages and disadvantages.

Advantages: operation develops its own system so that the speed and carrying capacity can be fully used.

Disadvantages: large quantities of work, problems of connecting with city centers.

（3）Applicable condition.

Megacities with large passenger capacity.

3. 既有线并列修建高铁客运专线

（1）定义。

与既有线并行，与既有线走向一致。既有中低速列车，也有高速列车。

（2）优缺点。

优点：工程量相对较小，不对城市造成分割，车站占地少。

缺点：换乘问题不易解决。

（3）适用条件。

客流量大、跨线客流少的状况。

3. Parallel Construction of High Speed Passenger Dedicated Line on Existing Railway

（1）Definition.

Parallel with and consistent with the exsiting lines. There are not only medium and low speed trains，but also high speed trains.

（2）Advantages and disadvantages.

Advantages：Relatively small quantities of work，no division of city，high degree of operation and less station space.

Disadvantages：It is not easy to solve the transfer problem.

（3）Applicable condition.

Large passenger flow and less cross-line passenger flow.

模块三　课堂练习

问题 1：查查你所在的城市高铁线路是以哪种方式修建的。

问题 2：思考货运线路为什么一般不进行由既有线到高速铁路的改造。

Module 3　In-class Exercises

Question 1: Find out the construction mode of high speed railway line in your city.

Question 2: Think about why not reconstruct existing freight line into high speed railway.

课堂练习

In-class Exercises

模块四　课后拓展

通过学到的知识总结高速铁路修建的模式有哪些，并说明不同模式的优缺点。

Module 4　After-class Activity

Summarize the construction mode of high speed railway and list their advantages and disadvantages respectively after study.

课后拓展

After-class Activity

任务三　高速铁路车站与线路设计的特点及趋势

Task 3　Design Features and Trends of High Speed Railway Station and Line

模块一　学前准备

在有可能的情况下，分别去当地的火车站和高铁站走走。

Module 1　Preparation before Class

Go to see the local railway station and high speed railway station，respectively.

课前学习笔记
Study Notes before Class

模块二　课堂学习

Module 2　In-class Learning

知识点一：高速铁路车站设计的特点

Key Point 1：Design Features of High Speed Railway Station

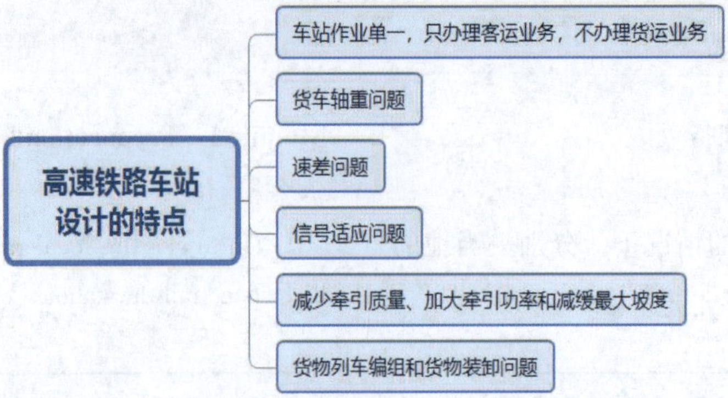

车站作业单一，只办理客运业务，不办理货运业务 single station operation with passenger service only，but no freight service

货车轴重问题 freight car axle load　速差问题 speed difference　信号适应问题 signal adaptation

减少牵引质量、加大牵引功率和减缓最大坡度 reduce tractive tonnage，increase traction power and slow down the maximum gradient

货物列车编组和货物装卸问题 freight train marshalling，goods loading and unloading

图 1–2　高速铁路车站设计的特点

Figure 1–2　Design Features of High Speed Railway Station

高速旅客不办理行包和邮件装卸业务（无行李车厢）。

高速铁路车站办理行包、邮件承运业务，必须建立地下拖车道路系统。这将大量增加高速铁路车站特别是部分高架于既有站上和与既有站并列设置的高速站的工程投资。

在高速列车和跨线快速列车上挂邮车和行包车而非两节旅客车厢的成本高，不经济。

为办理行包、邮件装卸而延长旅客

High speed passengers do not handle baggage or mail items （no baggage car）.

Underground trailer road system must be set up in high speed railway station to handle baggage and mail transportation. This will greatly increase the project investment of high speed stations，especially those are elevated or paralleled with the existing stations.

It is costly to take a postal car and a baggage car instead of two passenger cars on high speed train and cross–line express train.

Increasing stopping time of passenger trains to handle baggage or mail items runs counter to the shortest travel time pursued by

列车停站时间与高速铁路追求最短的旅行时间是背道而驰的。

high speed railways.

知识点二：高速铁路线路设计的特点

（1）高速铁路线路因设计时速高，应尽量采用较高的技术标准，选线应尽量短、顺、直，以修建桥、隧为主。

（2）速度标准高，各种设计参数（最小曲线半径、最大坡度、最大坡长、限界等）要求较高。

Key Point 2：Design Features of High Speed Railway Line

（1）Due to the high design speed of high speed railway line，higher technical standards should be adopted. The selected route should be short，smooth and straight，mainly with the construction of bridges and tunnels.

（2）High speed standard and various design parameters（minimum curve radius，maximum gradient，maximum slope length，clearance，etc）are very high.

模块三　课堂练习

Module 3　In-class Exercises

想一想，在设计时速 250 千米的高速铁路线路上，开行最高时速 100 千米的货运列车会造成哪些影响？

Think about the impact of running a freight train with top speed of 100km/h on a high speed line with design speed of 250km/h?

课堂练习
In-class Exercises

模块四　课后拓展

用学习的知识简述未来高速铁路在站场设计和建设中的发展趋势。

Module 4　After-class Activity

Make a brief description about the future developing trend of high speed railway in yard design and construction.

课后拓展

After-class Activity

项目二　高速铁路选线与主要技术标准

Project 2　Route Selection and Main Technical Standards for High Speed Railway

任务一　高速铁路选线的基本原则

Task 1　Basic Principles of Route Selection for High Speed Railway

模块一　学前准备

Module 1　Preparation before Class

请查阅资料，了解铁路选线的基本依据有哪些。

Do research and find out the fundamental basis for railway route selection.

课前学习笔记
Study Notes before Class

模块二　课堂学习

知识点一：铁路选线

1. 什么是铁路选线

铁路选线是指在铁路线路的控制点间，根据运输的需要和自然条件，选出经济上合理、技术上可行的最佳线路建设方案的过程及所涉及的技术。其任务是确定线路的平面位置和纵断面位置，并确定车站和各种铁路建筑的分布。

2. 铁路选线的步骤和手段

选线步骤分为：踏勘、初测、定测等。

铁路选线涉及多种专业，伴有大量野外工作和室内的研究、分析、计算工作。近年来在铁路选线中逐步采用了许多新的技术，如航测、卫星遥感摄影、数字地面模型、全息地震仪以及利用计算机的智能选线技术、自动绘图和预（概）算自动编制等。

Module 2　In-class Learning

Key Point 1：Railway Route Selection

1. What is Railway Route Selection

Railway route selection refers to the process and technologies involved in selecting the best economically reasonable and technically feasible route construction scheme between controlling points of railway lines according to transportation needs and natural conditions. The task of railway route selection is to determine the plane position and profile position of lines，as well as the distribution of stations and various railway the buildings.

2. Procedure and Method of Railway Route Selection

Railway route selection procedure includes make a field survey，preliminary survey，location survey，etc.

Railway route selection involves many specialties，accompanied by a lot of field work and indoor research，analysis and calculation. In recent years，many new technologies have been gradually adopted in railway route selection，e.g，aerial photogrammetry，satellite remote sensing photography，digital terrain model，holographic seismograph，computer-based intelligent route selection technology，automatic plotting，automatic budget preparation，etc.

知识点二：高速铁路选线的基本原则

高速铁路选线的基本原则主要包括以下五个方面：

1. 效益原则

主要考虑企业和国家的经济效益。

2. 兼容原则

线路走向宜靠近既有线，车站应尽量靠近接轨客运站。在困难情况下距离较远时应设联络线，区间线路应尽量取直、短。

3. 速度原则

平均速度与速度目标值的比值：一般地段大于0.9，困难地段宜大于0.85。必须综合研究地形条件和工程情况确定速度目标值，以避免标准的不合理和工程投资浪费。

4. 安全原则

选线和工程措施都必须考虑保证行车安全，不能遗留威胁安全的隐患。线路应尽量绕避不良地质地带，避免浸水路堤和洪水冲刷路堤。个别工点不能绕避时，需要采取保证安全的工程措施。

Key Point 2: Basic Principles of High Speed Railway Route Selection

Basic principles of route selection for high speed railway mainly include the following five aspects:

1. Benefit Principle

Mainly about economic benefits of enterprises and countries.

2. Compatibility Principle

Route direction should be close to the existing lines, and stations shall be close to the passenger junction station. In case of difficulty and far distance, a connecting line shall be set up. Interval lines shall be straight and short.

3. Speed Principle

Ratio of average speed to target speed: general section>0.9 and difficult section>0.85. Target speed value must be determined through comprehensive study of terrain conditions and engineering situation to avoid unreasonable standards and project investment waste.

4. Safety Principle

Driving safety must be taken into consideration for route selection and engineering measures. Meanwhile, hidden dangers that threaten safety cannot be left. Route selection should avoid poor geological zones to avoid immersible embankment and flooded embankment. When it cannot be avoided, engineering measures shall be taken to ensure safety.

5. 舒适原则

高速铁路选线应尽量采用较高的技术标准，满足列车运行速度和旅客舒适度的要求。影响舒适度的因素包括线路设计参数、车辆性能、线路的整体刚度等。

5. Comfort Principle

High speed railway route worksites it selection should adopt higher technical standards to meet the requirements of train speed and passenger comfort. Factors that affect comfort include route design parameters，vehicle performance，route overall rigidity，etc.

表 2-1 高速铁路选线的基本原则

Chart 2-1 Basic Principles of High Speed Railway Route Selection

效益原则	主要考虑企业财务效益和国民经济效益。
兼容原则	线路走向宜靠近既有线，车站应尽量靠近接轨客运站，困难情况下距离较远时应设联络线，区间线路应尽量取直、短。
速度原则	平均速度与速度目标值的比值：一般地段＞ 0.9, 困难地段宜＞ 0.85 。必须综合研究地形条件和工程情况确定速度目标值，以避免标准的不合理和工程投资浪费。
安全原则	选线和工程措施都必须考虑保证行车的安全，不能遗留造成威胁安全的隐患。线路应尽量绕避不良地质地带，避免浸水路堤和洪水冲刷路堤。个别工点不能绕避时，需要采取保证安全的工程措施。
舒适原则	高速铁路选线应尽量采用较高的技术标准，满足列车运行速度和旅客舒适度的要求。影响舒适度的因素包括线路设计参数、车辆性能、线路的整体刚度等。

效益原则 benefit principle 主要考虑企业财务效益和国民经济效益。Mainly about financial benefits of enterprises and national economic benefits. 兼容原则 compatibility principle 线路走向宜靠近既有线，车站应尽量靠近接轨客运站，困难情况下距离较远时应设联络线，区间线路应尽量取直、短。Route direction should be close to existing lines, and stations shall be close to the passenger junction station. In case of difficulty and far distance, a connecting line shall be set up. Interval lines shall be straight and short. 速度原则 speed principle 平均速度与速度目标值的比值：一般地段＞ 0.9, 困难地段宜＞ 0.85 。必须综合研究地形条件和工程情况确定速度目标值，以避免标准的不合理和工程投资浪费。Ratio of average speed to target speed: general section ＞ 0.9 and difficult section ＞ 0.85. Target speed value must be determined through comprehensive study of terrain conditions and engineering situation to avoid unreasonable standards and project investment waste. 安全原则 safety principle 选线和工程措施都必须考虑保证行车的安全，不能遗留造成威胁安全的隐患。线路应尽量绕避不良地质地带，避免浸水路堤和洪水冲刷路堤。个别工点不能绕避时，需要采取保证安全的工程措施。Driving safety must be taken into consideration for route selection and engineering measures. Meanwhile, hidden dangers that threaten safety cannot be left. Route selection should avoid poor geological zones to avoid immersible embankment and flooded embankment. When it cannot be avoided, engineering measures shall be taken to ensure safety. 舒适原则 comfort principle 高速铁路选线应尽量采用较高的技术标准，满足列车运行速度和旅客舒适度的要求。影响舒适度的因素包括线路设计参数、车辆性能、线路的整体刚度等。High speed railway route selection should adopt higher technical standards to meet the requirements of train speed and passenger comfort. Factors that affect comfort include route design parameters, vehicle performance, route overall rigidity, etc.

学习笔记

Study Notes

模块三　课堂练习

根据已学知识判断以下语句体现了高速铁路选线的什么原则。

（1）这条线路的走向应该和原线路一致。

（2）线路如走这个地方，那么路堤容易浸水。

（3）A 方案明显比 B 方案节省资金。

Module 3　In-class Exercises

According to what you have learned, choose the correct principle for the following sentences about high speed railway route selection.

(1) The direction of this route should be the same as the original one.

(2) If the route goes this way, the embankment will be easily immersed.

(3) Scheme A is obviously more economical than Scheme B.

课堂练习
In-class Exercises

模块四　课后拓展

请思考高速铁路选线与普通铁路有什么不同。

Module 4　After-class Activity

Think about the differences of route selection between high speed railway and ordinary railway.

课后拓展

After-class Activity

任务二　铁路线路的分类分级

Task 2　Classification and Grade of Railway Line

模块一　学前准备

Module 1　Preparation before Class

预习铁路分类部分的内容，上网找一张铁路线路的图片，并判断它是什么类型的线路。

Preview the classification of railway parts, find a railway line picture on the Internet and decide its type.

课前学习笔记
Study Notes before Class

模块二　课堂学习

Module 2　In-class Learning

知识点一：铁路的分类

Key Point 1: Classification of Railway

1. 按线路作用分类

1. Classification by the function of Line

（1）正线指连接车站并贯穿或直股伸入车站的线路。

(1) Main line refers to the line linking station or passing through station.

图 2-1　正线

Figure 2-1　Main Line

（2）侧线指侧向通过车站的线路。

(2) Side line refers to the line passing through station laterally.

图 2-2　侧线

Figure 2-2　Side Line

（3）折返线是在终点站或者中间站，为方便列车掉头、转线、存车而设置的线路。之字形铁路便是其中之一。

（3）Turnaround track is at the terminal station or intermediate station to facilitate trains to turn around，shunt and store cars. Zigzag railway is one of them.

图 2–3　之字形铁路

Figure 2–3　Zigzag Railway

（4）渡线是在上下正线之间（或者其他平行线路之间）设置的连接线。

（4）Crossover line is set between upper and lower main lines （or between other parallel lines） as connecting line.

图 2–4　渡线

Figure 2–4　Crossover Line

（5）停车线是场内作业停放列车的线路。

（5）Parking track is used for parking trains in the field.

图 2-5 停车线

Figure 2-5 Parking Track

（6）检修线是设在车辆基地检修库内，专门用于检修列车，设有地沟、车架设备和检修设备的线路。

（6）Repair track is located in maintenance warehouse of the vehicle base and is specially used for train maintenance. It is equipped with trench, frame device and maintenance equipment.

图 2-6 检修线

Figure 2-6 Repair Track

（7）试验线是设在车辆基地，用于对检修完毕的列车进行状态检测的线路。

（7）Test line is set up at vehicle base to test condition of the overhauled train.

图 2-7 试验线

Figure 2-7 Test Line

（8）出入场线是连接车站和正线的线路。

（8）Entrance-exit line connects station with main line.

图 2-8 出入场线

Figure 2-8 Entrance-exit Line

（9）联络线是为调动列车作业而设置的线路。

（9）Connecting line is set up for train shunting operation.

图 2-9　联络线

Figure 2-9　Connecting Line

2. 按线路正线数目分类

2. Classification by the Number of Main Line

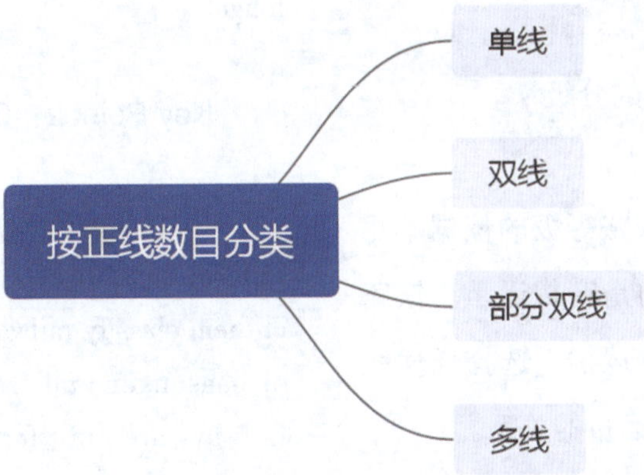

按正线数目分类 classification by the number of main line

单线 single line　双线 double lines　部分双线 partial double lines　多线 multi lines

图 2-10　按正线数目分类

Figure 2-10　Classification by the Number of Main Line

3. 按线路允许的最高行车速度分类

3. Classification by the Maximum Running Speed Allowed on the Line

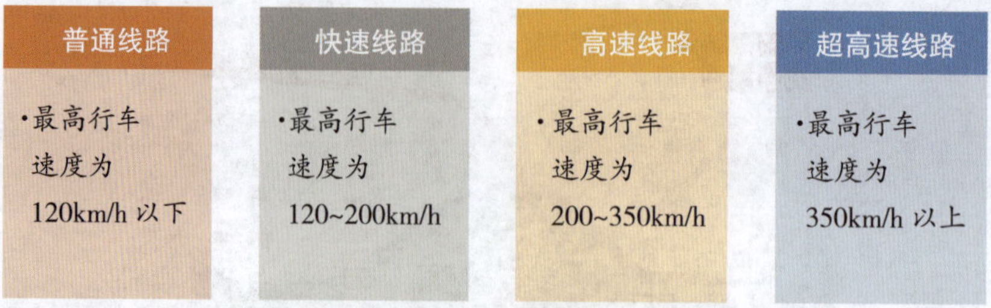

普通线路 ordinary line　最高行车速度为 120km/h 以下 maximum driving speed：120km/h or less
快速线路 fast speed line　最高行车速度为 120~200km/h maximum driving speed：120~200km/h
高速线路 high speed line　最高行车速度为 200~350km/h maximum driving speed：200~350km/h
超高速线路 super high speed line　最高行车速度为 350km/h 以上 maximum driving speed：350km/h or more

图 2-11　按线路允许的最高行车速度分类

Figure 2-11　Classification by the Maximum Running Speed Allowed on the Line

此外，按钢轨连接方式的不同，铁路线路可分为普通线路和无缝线路；按运行列车种类的不同，铁路线路可分为客运专线、货运专线和客货混跑线路。

In addition, it can be divided into ordinary track and continuously welded rail track (CWR track) by different rail connection modes. According to types of trains, they can be divided into passenger dedicated line, freight dedicated line and railway of mixed service for passenger and freight.

知识点二：铁路的分级

Key Point 2：Grade of Railway

世界各国划定铁路等级的依据不尽相同，但大多根据的是客货运量。铁路的修建都是为了客货运输，选择任何线路参数都不能脱离与运量的关系。

中国铁路共划分为四个等级，即Ⅰ级、Ⅱ级、Ⅲ级和Ⅳ级，具体条件见表 2-2。

Different countries have different criteria for railway classification, but most of them classify railways according to volume of passenger and freight traffic. Because railways are built for passenger and freight transportation, any route parameter cannot be out of traffic volume.

Railways in China are divided into four grades, namely Class Ⅰ, Ⅱ, Ⅲ and Ⅳ, see Chart 2-2.

表 2-2　铁路等级

Chart 2-2　Grade of Railway

铁路等级	铁路在路网中的意义	近年客货运量 /Mt
Ⅰ级	在铁路网中起骨干作用	≥ 20
Ⅱ级	在铁路网中起联络、辅助作用	< 20 且≥ 10
Ⅲ级	为某一区域或企业服务	< 10 且≥ 5
Ⅳ级	为某一地区或企业服务	< 5

铁路等级 grade of railway　铁路在路网中的意义 significance of railway in the road network　近年客货运量 /Mt passenger and freight volume in recent years /Mt　Ⅰ级 class Ⅰ railway　在铁路网中起骨干作用 play a trunk role in railway network　Ⅱ级 class Ⅱ railway　在铁路网中起联络、辅助作用 play a linking and auxiliary role in railway network　<20 且≥10 < 20 and ≥10　Ⅲ级 class Ⅲ railway　为某一区域或企业服务 serve for a certain region or enterprise　< 10 且≥5 <10 and ≥5　Ⅳ级 class Ⅳ railway　为某一地区或企业服务 serve for a certain region or enterprise

注：Mt：百万吨。

Note：Mt （Million ton）.

学习笔记

Study Notes

模块三　课堂练习

Module 3　In-class Exercises

图 2-12（a）和图 2-12（b）是北京轨道交通线路的一部分，试判断：按照作用分类，它们分别属于哪种线路？

Figure 2-12（a）and Figure 2-12（b）are part of rail transit lines in Beijing. Decide the type of line by its functional classification, respectively.

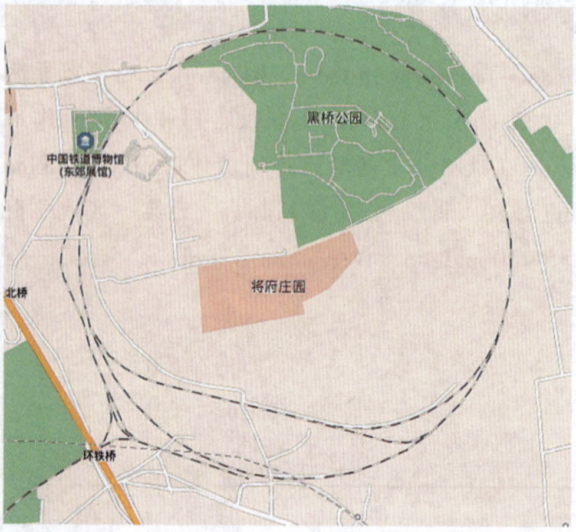

图 2-12（a）
Figure 2-12（a）

图 2-12（b）
Figure 2-12（b）

课堂练习
In-class Exercises

模块四　课后拓展

思考：如按线路允许的最高行车速度分类，地铁线路都是普通线路吗？

Module 4　After-class Activity

Think about are all subway lines the ordinary lines if lines are classified by their maximum running speed?

课后拓展

After-class Activity

任务三　主要技术标准的选择

Task 3　Selection of Main Technical Standards

模块一　学前准备

查找相关资料，了解铁路各主要技术标准的含义。

Module 1　Preparation before Class

Search relevant materials to understand the meaning of main technical standards of railway.

课前学习笔记

Study Notes before Class

模块二　课堂学习

Module 2　In-class Learning

知识点一：铁路技术标准

Key Point 1：Railway Technical Standards

修建一条铁路之前，需要对其采用的技术标准进行限定。

铁路的技术标准有很多，主要包括：正线数目、限制坡度、最小曲线半径、到发线有效长度、闭塞类型、牵引种类、机车类型、机车交路和车站分布等。

Before building a railway，it is necessary to set technical standards. There are many technical standards for railways，mainly include number of main lines，ruling grade，minimum curve radius，effective lengths of receiving-departure track，block type，traction type，type of locomotive，locomotive routing，station distribution，etc.

1. 正线数目

连接车站并贯穿或直股伸入车站的线路为正线。正线的数量即正线数目。

1. Number of Main Line

Refers to lines linking station or passing through station. The number of main line is the amount of main lines.

2. 限制坡度

列车上、下坡运行都要求坡道的坡度不能过大。在一个区段上，决定一台某一类型机车所能牵引的货物列车重量（最大值）的坡度，叫作限制坡度。

2. Ruling Grade

The grade must not be too large when the train goes up or down a slope. In a section，the maximum gradient of a single locomotive hauling（maximum value）is defined as ruling grade.

3. 最小曲线半径

为了减小离心力，保证列车运行安全、平稳和旅客的舒适，必须限制铁路曲线部分的最小半径不能低于某个值。

3. Minimum Curve Radius

In order to reduce centrifugal force to ensure train safety and passenger comfort. The minimum radius of railway curve cannot be lower than a certain value.

4. 到发线有效长度

指能停放货物列车而不影响相邻股道作业的最大长度。

4. Effective Length of Receiving-Departure Track

Refers to the maximum length that can be used for freight train parking without influencing the operation on adjacent line.

5. 闭塞类型

主要有自动闭塞、半自动闭塞和自动站间闭塞三类。

5. Block Type

Mainly includes automatic block，semi-automatic block and automatic block among stations.

6. 牵引种类

主要包括电力、内燃、蒸汽三种。

6. Traction Type

Mainly includes electric traction，diesel traction and steam traction.

知识点二：铁路技术标准的选择

铁路技术标准对铁路的运输能力、工程造价、工程标准、运营质量等都有重大影响。因此，铁路的主要技术标准应综合考虑多方面因素，慎重确定。

Key Point 2：Selection of Railway Technical Standards

Railway technical standards have great influence on traffic capacity，construction cost，project standards，and operation quality，etc. Therefore，the main technical standards for railway should be carefully determined with comprehensive consideration.

表 2-3　主要铁路技术标准

Chart 2-3　Main Railway Technical Standards

最小曲线半径	车辆段最小曲线半径的确定，是综合考虑车辆的转向架型式、工程的可实施性、工程与运营的经济性、环境影响等各个方面平衡的结果。
到发线有效长度	一条铁路线路旅客列车和货物列车的到发线有效长度取决于该线所属铁路等级、输送能力、地形条件等因素，同时也与相邻线路到发线有效长度有关。
限制坡度	与铁路能力有直接关系，故应根据铁路等级、地形、牵引动力条件、运量及邻接铁路的牵引定数等因素，在初步设计中分析比较，慎重选定。

最小曲线半径 minimum curve radius　车辆段最小曲线半径的确定，是综合考虑车辆的转向架型式、工程的可实施性、工程与运营的经济性、环境影响等各个方面平衡的结果。Minimum curve radius of car depot depends on comprehensive consideration of various factors, e.g. bogie type of vehicle, feasibility of project, economy of project and operation, environmental influence, etc.　到发线有效长度 available length of arrival and departure line　一条铁路线路旅客列车和货物列车的到发线有效长度取决于该线所属铁路等级、输送能力、地形条件等因素，同时也与相邻线路到发线有效长度有关。Available length of arrival and departure line of passenger train and freight train on a railway line depends on factors as the grades of railways, carrying capacity, terrain conditions, etc. It is also related to the available length of arrival and departure line of adjacent lines.　限制坡度 ruling grade　与铁路能力有直接关系，故应根据铁路等级、地形、牵引动力条件、运量及邻接铁路的牵引定数等因素，在初步设计中分析比较，慎重选定。It is directly related to traffic capacity, so it shall be carefully selected after analysis and comparison in the preliminary design according to factors as the grades of railways, terrain conditions, traction power conditions, and coordination with tonnage rating of adjacent railways, etc.

学习笔记

Study Notes

模块三　课堂练习

假设一辆机车能通过的最小曲线半径为 80 米，该机车运行路线的最小曲线半径不能低于多少？

Module 3　In-class Exercises

Suppose a locomotive vehicle can pass through a minimum curve radius of 80 m, what is the minimum curve radius of the route?

课堂练习

In-class Exercises

模块四　课后拓展

上网查找资料，了解某一段铁路的具体技术标准。

Module 4　After-class Activity

Search online to understand the specific technical standards for a certain section of railway.

课后拓展

After-class Activity

项目三　高速铁路线路平面及纵断面设计

Project 3　Plane and Profile Design for High Speed Railway

任务一　线路平面

Task 1　Railway Plane

模块一　学前准备

查阅资料，了解高速铁路线路平面的组成要素。

Module 1　Preparation before Class

Search information to understand the components of plane of high speed railway line.

课前学习笔记

Study Notes before Class

模块二　课堂学习

Module 2　In-class Learning

线路的平面是指线路中心线在水平面上的投影，它表明线路的曲、直变化状态和走向。线路的平面由直线、圆曲线以及连接直线与圆曲线的缓和曲线组成。线路在空间的位置是用它的中心线来表示的。线路中心线是指距外轨半个轨距的铅垂线与两路肩边缘水平连线交点的纵向连线。为了满足沿途客流的需要、躲避障碍，在线路向前延伸的过程中就不得不出现曲直变化。因此，线路平面的组成要素就包括直线和曲线。

Railway plane refers to projection of the track centerline on horizontal position. It indicates the curved and straight changes and track alignment. Railway plane consists of straight line，circular curve and transition curve connecting straight line and circular curve. The location of line in space is indicated by its centerline. Track centerline refers to the longitudinal connecting line between the vertical line half a track gauge from the outer rails and the intersection of horizontal connecting lines at edge of two shoulders. To meet the needs of passenger flow along the line and bypassing obstacles，there will be curved and straight changes in the process of route extending. Therefore，the components of plane are straight line and curve.

知识点一：曲线

Key Point 1：Curve

线路在转向处所设的曲线为圆曲线，其基本组成要素有：曲线半径 R、曲线转角 α，曲线长 L、切线长度 T，如图 3-1 所示。

The curve sets at the turning point of railway line is a circular curve，and its basic elements include curve radius R，curve angle α，curve length L and tangent length T，as shown in Figure 3-1.

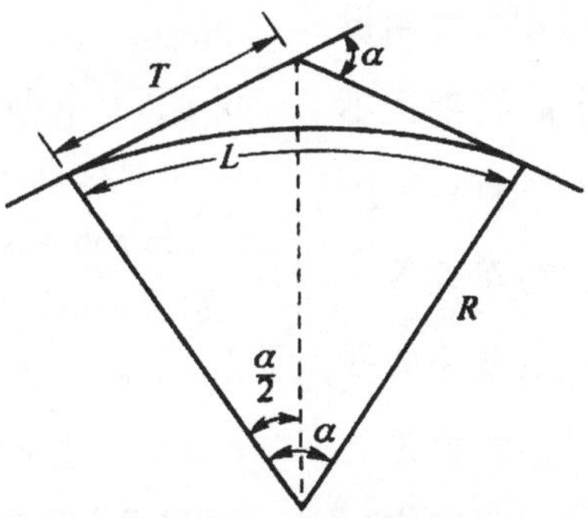

图 3-1　圆曲线要素

Figure 3-1　Elements of Circular Curve

在线路设计时，一般是先设计出 α 和 R，再按下式计算出 T 及 L：

$$T = R \cdot \tan\frac{\alpha}{2}$$

$$L = \frac{\pi}{180} \cdot R \cdot \alpha$$

式中：

T——切线长度，米；

R——曲线半径，米；

α——曲线转角，度；

L——曲线长，米。

曲线半径越大，行车速度越高，但工程量越大，工程费用越高。

小半径曲线地段需要适当限速运行。当列车通过曲线时，为了提高运营安全性与乘客的舒适性，在圆曲线地段应根据曲线半径和实测行车速度，在曲线外股钢轨上合理设置超高 H（单位为毫米）。$H=11.8v^2/R$（v 为列车平均运行速度，单位：千米/时），曲线超高一经设定则不能任意调整。

线路直线与圆曲线往往不是直接相连的，中间要加一段缓和曲线。曲线半径的最小值与设计速度密切相关，当设计时速为 300 千米时，最小曲线半径不能小于 4500 米。为了使列车按规定速度安全、平稳运行，需要根据行车速度、车辆轮对有关尺寸等因素规定线路曲线的最小半径。线路曲线半径最小值是高速铁路主要技术标准之一，根据国家标准《高速铁路设计规范》（TB 10621—

In line design，α and R are generally designed first，then T and L can be calculated by the following formula：

$$T = R \cdot \tan\frac{\alpha}{2}$$

$$L = \frac{\pi}{180} \cdot R \cdot \alpha$$

Where

T—tangent length，m;

R—curve radius，m;

α —curve angle，°；

L— curve length，m.

The larger the curve radius，the higher the driving speed. The larger the engineering quantity，the higher the construction cost.

It is necessary to run at a limited speed in section with small-radius curve. When train passes through curve，in order to improve operation safety and riding comfort for passengers，the superelevation H. $H = 11.8v^2/R$（mm）（v is the average train running speed，km/h） should be reasonably set in the outer rail of curve according to curve radius and measured running speed in circular curve section. The superelevation of curve cannot be adjusted at random.

Straight line and circular curve are not directly connected，a transition curve should be added in the middle. Minimum curve radius is closely related to the design speed. When the design speed is 300km/h，the minimum curve radius cannot be less than 4500m. To ensure that the train runs safely and smoothly at a specified speed，it is necessary to specify the minimum curve radius according to factors as running speed and relevant size of wheels. The

2014）规定，线路平面最小曲线半径应符合表 3-1、表 3-2 的规定。

minimum curve radius of line is one of the main technical standards for high speed railway. According to the national standard of "Code for Design of High Speed Railway"（TB 10621-2014），the minimum curve radius of line plane shall comply with the provisions in Chart 3-1 and Chart 3-2.

1. 与设计速度匹配的平面曲线半径应符合表 3-1 的规定

1. Curve Radius of Plane Matching the Design Speed shall Comply with Provisions in Chart 3-1

表 3-1　平面曲线半径表

Chart 3-1　Curve Radius of Plane

设计速度（千米 / 时）			350	300	250
最小值（米）	有砟轨道	一般	7000	5000	3500
		困难	6000	4500	3000
	无砟轨道	一般	7000	5000	3200
		困难	5500	4000	2800
最大值（米）			12000		

设计速度（千米 / 时）design speed（km/h）　最小值（米）minimum value（m）　有砟轨道 ballasted track　无砟轨道 ballastless track　一般 general　困难 difficult　最大值（米）maximum value（m）

注：

（1）困难最小值应进行技术和经济比选后采用。

（2）车站两端减、加速地段的最小曲线半径应结合行车速度曲线合理选用。

Note:

（1）Minimum difficult value shall be adopted after the technical and economic comparison.

（2）Minimum curve radius of the deceleration and acceleration sections at both ends of station shall be reasonably selected in combination with the driving speed curve.

2. 车站两端减、加速地段的最小曲线半径应结合行车速度曲线合理选用

2. The Minimum Curve Radius of Deceleration and Acceleration Sections at both Ends of the Station should be Reasonably Selected in Combination with the Driving Speed Curve

表 3-2　限速地段曲线半径表

Chart 3-2　Curve Radius in Speed-Limit Zone

行车速度（千米 / 时）	200	160	120	80
一般最小值（米）	2200	1600	1000	600
困难最小值（米）	2000	1400	800	400

行车速度（千米 / 时）running speed（km/h）　一般最小值（米）general minimum value（m）
困难最小值（米）difficult minimum value（m）

注：困难最小值应进行技术和经济比选后采用。

Note: Minimum difficult value shall be adopted after the technical and economic comparison.

知识点二：缓和曲线

Key Point 2：Transition Curve

为保证列车安全，使线路平顺地由直线过渡到圆曲线，或由圆曲线过渡到直线，以避免离心力的突然产生和消除，常需要在直线与圆曲线之间设置一个曲率半径变化的曲线，这个曲线被称为缓和曲线。图 3-2 所示为设有缓和曲线的线路。

To ensure train safety and make a smooth line transit from a straight line to circular curve or from a circular curve to straight line，it is often necessary to set a curve with variation in radius of curvature between straight line and circular curve to avoid sudden generation or elimination of centrifugal force. This kind of curve is called a transition curve. Line with transition curve is shown in Figure 3-2.

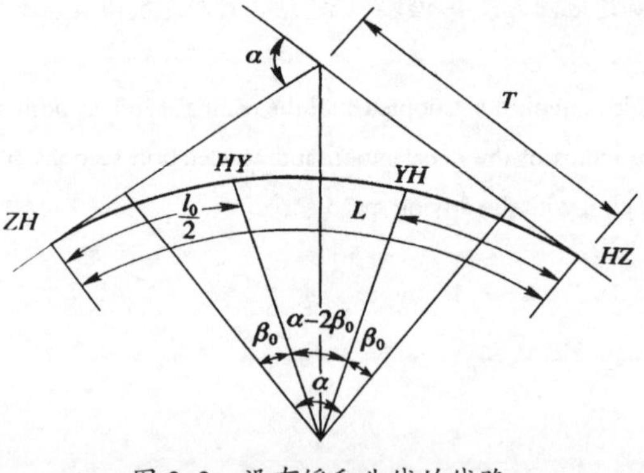

图 3-2　设有缓和曲线的线路

Figure 3-2　Line with Transition Curve

缓和曲线的特征为：从缓和曲线所衔接的直线一端起，它的曲率半径 ρ 由无穷大逐渐减小到它所衔接的圆曲线半径 R。它可以使离心力逐渐增加或减小，不致造成到车横向强烈摇摆，这对改善运营条件、保证行车安全和平顺都有很大的作用，如图 3-3 所示。

Transition curve is characterized in that from the end of straight line to which the transition curve connects, its radius of curvature ρ gradually decreases from infinity to circular curve radius R it connects. Transition curve can gradually increase or decrease centrifugal force without causing strong horizontal sway of vehicle, which plays a great role in improving operating conditions and ensuring driving safety, as shown in Figure 3-3.

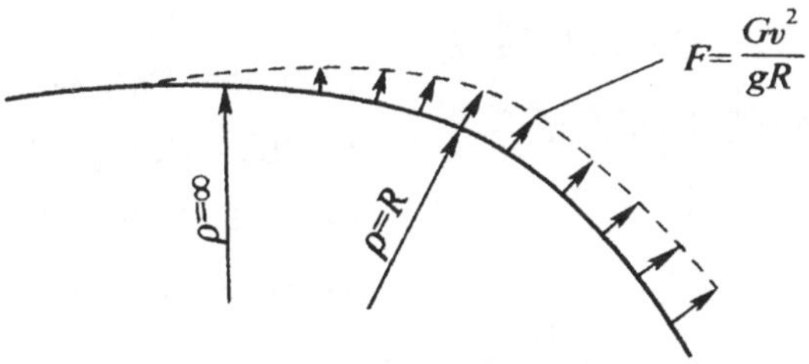

图 3-3　离心力变化示意图

Figure 3-3　Schematic Diagram of Centrifugal Force Variation

比如，《高速铁路设计规范》（TB 10621—2014）规定：当设计时速为 300 千米、曲线半径为 10000 米的时候，其缓和曲线长度为 220~270 米。

For example, "Code for Design of High Speed Railway" (TB 10621-2014) stipulates that when the design speed is 300km and curve radius is 10000m, the length of transition curve is 220~270m.

知识点三：夹直线与线间距

Key Point 3: Tangent between Curves and Track Spacing

两相邻曲线，转向相同，称为同向曲线；转向相反，称为反向曲线。两条相邻曲线间应设置一定长度的直线，以保证列车平稳运行。若车辆运行在同向曲线上，因相邻曲线半径及超高高度不同，故车体内倾斜度不同；若车辆运行

Two adjacent curves with the same turning direction are called curves in the same direction. If the two turn to opposite are called reverse curves. A straight line with certain length shall be set between two adjacent curves to ensure smooth train operation. If trains run on curves in the same direction,

在反向曲线上，因两曲线超高方向不同，故车体时而向左倾斜，时而向右倾斜。这两种情况都会造成车体摇晃震动。为了保证运营安全，提供平稳的行车条件，不宜设置连续曲线，并且必须保证曲线之间有足够长度的夹直线。

the inclination in vehicle body is different due to different radiuses and superelevation of adjacent curves. If trains run on the reverse curve, the vehicle body inclines to left or right due to different superelevation directions of two curves. Both situations will cause shake and vibration of vehicle body. To ensure safe operation and stable driving condition, it is not appropriate to set continuous curves on line. It is also necessary to ensure enough tangent between curves.

1. 两相邻曲线间的夹直线和两缓和曲线间的圆曲线最小长度应符合表3-3的规定

1. The Minimal Length of Tangent between Two Adjacent Curves and the Circular Curve between Two Transition Curves shall Comply with Provisions in Chart 3-3.

表3-3　圆曲线或夹直线最小长度

Chart 3-3　Minimum Length of Circular Curve or Tangent between Curves

设计速度（千米/时）	200	160	80
圆曲线或夹直线最小长度（米）	2200	1600	600

设计速度（千米/时）design speed（km/h）　圆曲线或夹直线最小长度（米）minimum length of circular curve or tangent between curves（m）

2. 正线上的道岔与缓和曲线间的直线段最小长度应符合表3-4的规定

2. The Minimal Length of Straight Line between Turnout on Main Line and Transition Curve shall Comply with Provisions in Chart 3-4

表3-4　正线上的道岔与缓和曲线间的直线段最小长度

Chart 3-4　The Minimum Length of Straight Line between Turnout on Main Line and Transition Curves

设计速度（千米/时）	350	300	250
直线段最小长度（米）	210（170）	180（150）	150（120）

设计速度（千米/时）design speed（km/h）　直线段最小长度（米）minimum length of straight line（m）

3. 区间正线线间距应符合表3-5的规定

3. Track Spacing of Main Line in Section shall Comply with Provisions in Chart 3-5

表3-5 区间正线线间距

Chart 3-5 Track Spacing of Main Line in Section

设计速度（千米 / 时）	350	300	250
最小线间距（米）	5.0	4.8	4.6

设计速度（千米 / 时）design speed （km/h） 最小线间距（米）minimum track spacing （m）

学习笔记
Study Notes

模块三　课堂练习

问题 1：线路平面的组成要素有哪些？

问题 2：讨论在高速铁路线路平面中，其缓和曲线与夹直线最小长度受哪些因素影响。

Module 3　In-class Exercises

Question 1：What are the components of line plane?

Question 2：Discuss the factors affecting the minimum length of transition curve and tangent between curves in high speed railway line plane.

课堂练习

In-class Exercises

模块四　课后拓展

查阅和收集高速铁路设计规范和标准，学习和分析线路平面设计的相关规定。

Module 4　After-class Activity

Consult and collect design codes and standards for high speed railway. Learn and analyze the relevant provisions of line plane design.

课后拓展

After-class Activity

任务二　线路纵断面

Task 2　Line Profile

模块一　学前准备

Module 1　Preparation before Class

查阅资料，了解高速铁路线路纵断面的组成要素。

Search information to understand the components of line profile of high speed railway.

课前学习笔记

Study Notes before Class

模块二　课堂学习

知识点一：高速铁路纵断面的组成要素

为了适应地面的起伏，线路上除了平道以外，还修了不同的坡道。因此，平道与坡道就成了线路纵断面的组成要素。线路纵断面是指线路中心线展直后在铅垂面上的投影，表明线路的坡度变化。线路纵断面由平道、坡道及设于变坡点处的竖曲线组成。

坡道的陡与缓用坡度来表示。坡度是指坡道线路中心线与水平线夹角的正切值，如图 3-4 所示。坡道坡度的大小通常用千分率表示。

Module 2　In-class Learning

Key Point 1：Components of High Speed Railway Profile

To adapt to ups and downs of ground, in addition to flat roads, different slopes are built on line. Therefore, flat roads and slopes are the components of line profile. Line profile is the projection on vertical plane by spreading out track centerline, which indicates changes of gradient. Line profile consists of flat road, slope and vertical curve at the point of gradient change.

Steep slopes and gentle slopes are indicated by gradient. Gradient is the tangent value the angle α between slope track centerline and horizontal line, as shown in Figure 3-4. Gradient is usually expressed in permillage.

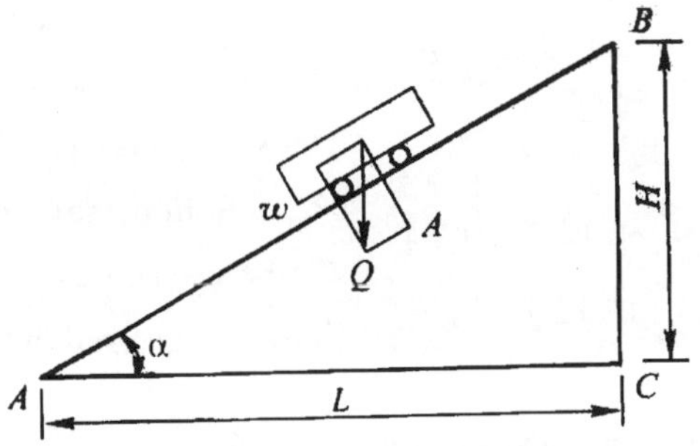

图 3-4　坡道与坡道阻力示意图

Figure 3-4　Schematic Diagram of Slope and Gradient Resistance

式中：

$$i = \frac{H}{L} = \tan\alpha$$

i——坡度值，‰；

α——坡道线路中心线与水平线夹角，度。

Where

$$i = \frac{H}{L} = \tan\alpha$$

i—gradient value，‰；

α—angle between slope track centerline and horizontal line，°.

例如，若 L 为 1500 米，H 为 9 米，则 AB 坡道的坡度为 6‰。

有了坡道，给列车运行带来了不良的影响。列车在坡道上运行时，会受到一种由坡道引起的阻力，这一阻力被称为坡道附加阻力。从图 3-4 中可以看出，列车所受重力 Q 可以分解为垂直于坡道的分力 A 和平行于坡道的分力 w。前一个分力由轨道的反作用力所抵消，后一个分力 w 就成为坡道附加阻力。

$$w=Q\cdot\sin\alpha\approx Q\cdot\tan\alpha=Q\cdot i$$

式中：

i——坡道的坡度。

列车平均每单位重量所受到的坡度阻力，叫作单位坡道阻力（w_i）。因此，

$$w_i=w/Q\times1000=Q\cdot i/Q\times1000=i\times1000$$

也就是说，列车每单位质量上坡时所受的坡道阻力（N/kN），等于用千分率表示的这一坡道度数。

列车上坡时，规定坡道阻力为“+”；而下坡时，规定坡道阻力为“-”。

坡度越大，列车上坡时的坡道阻力也就越大，同样牵引动力（在列车运行速度相同的条件下）所能牵引的列车质量也就越小。

For example，if L is 1500m and H is 9m，the gradient of AB slope is 6‰ .

Slopes often have negative impacts on train operation. When a train runs on a slope, it will encounter a kind of resistance caused by slope，which is called additional resistance for gradient. As we can see from Figure 3-4，the gravity Q on train can be divided into component force A vertical to slope and component force w parallel to slope. The former is counteracted by the counter force of track, and the latter becomes the additional resistance for gradient.

$$w=Q\cdot\sin\alpha\approx Q\cdot\tan\alpha=Q\cdot i$$

Where

i—gradient .

The average gradient resistance on per unit weight of train is called unit gradient resistance（w_i）. Therefore,

$$w_i=w/Q\times1000=Q\cdot i/Q\times1000=i\times1000$$

Thus，the gradient resistance（N/kN）for every unit mass of train going up is equal to the degree of slope expressed in permillage.

When train goes up，the gradient resistance is defined as “+” . When train goes down，the gradient resistance is defined as “-” .

The greater the gradient，the greater the gradient resistance when train goes up, the smaller the weight of train that can be pulled with the same traction power （under the condition of same running speed）.

知识点二：最大坡度和最小坡度

为了在列车牵引功率一定、运行速度一定的条件下，确保列车一定的运力，在线路纵断面设计时要对线路的最大程度进行限制，即设定最大坡度。

最大坡度是线路纵断面设计最重要的因素。最大坡度会影响到线路的工程造价和线路的行车条件。线路坡度选择得过小，就会大大增加工程量，加大其工程造价；最大坡度选择得过大，将不利于行车，并使线路的运输能力严重受限。

我国高速铁路在纵断面设计时兼顾行车安全、乘客舒适和速度要求，规定区间正线的最大坡度不宜大于20‰；在困难条件下经技术和经济比较后，则不应大于30‰。

为了满足纵向排水需要，隧道内坡道可设置为单面坡道或人字坡道。地下水发育的长隧道宜采用人字坡，坡度不应小于3‰。路堑地段线路的坡度不宜小于2‰。

站坪范围的正线坡度设计应符合下列规定：

（1）到发线有效长度范围内的正线应设在平道上，当设在坡道上时坡度不应大于1‰。

（2）越行站的正线坡度不宜大于6‰。

Key Point 2: Maximum Gradient and Minimum Gradient

To ensure the train traffic capacity under the condition of certain tractive power and running speed, it is necessary to limit the maximum degree of line during line profile design, i.e. the maximum gradient should be set.

Maximum gradient is the most important element in line profile design. Construction cost and running condition of line will be affected by maximum gradient. If the gradient is too small, it will greatly increase the project quantity and construction cost. If the maximum gradient is too large, it will go against train operation and severely limit traffic capacity.

When designing line profile for China's high speed railway, consideration should be given to running safety, passenger comfort and speed requirements. Maximum gradient of the main line in specified section should not be greater than 20‰ and it shall not be greater than 30‰ with technical and economic backwardness under difficult conditions.

To meet the needs of longitudinal drainage, slopes in tunnel can be set as one-way slope or herringbone slope. Herringbone slope should be adopted for long tunnels with groundwater, and the gradient shall not be less than 3‰. Gradient in cutting section should not be less than 2‰.

Gradient design of the main line in station site shall meet the following requirements:

(1) Main line within the effective length of arrival and departure line shall be set on flat roads. Gradient shall not be greater than 1‰ when set on slopes.

（3）车站咽喉区的正线坡度宜与到发线有效长度范围内的坡度一致。在困难条件下，始发站不宜大于 2.5‰、中间站不宜大于 6‰。

(2) The gradient of main line in overtaking station should not be greater than 6‰.

(3) The gradient of main line in station throat area should be consistent with the gradient in effective length of arrival and departure line. Under difficult conditions, the departure station should not be larger than 2.5 ‰ and the intermediate station should not be larger than 6‰.

知识点三：变坡点

Key Point 3: Point of Gradient Change

平道与坡道、坡道与坡道的交点，叫作变坡点。列车经过变坡点时，由于坡度的突然变化，车钩内产生附加应力。坡度变化越大，附加应力越大，容易造成断钩事故，如图 3-5 所示。为了保证列车的运行平稳和安全，规定正线相邻坡段的坡度大于或等于 1‰时，应采用竖曲线连接，如图 3-6 所示。

Intersections of flat road with slope, or slope with slope, is called point of gradient change. When train passes through point of gradient change, additional stress is generated in coupler due to the sudden change of gradient. The greater the gradient change, the greater the additional stress. It is easy to cause broken coupler accident, as shown in Figure 3-5. To ensure smooth and safe train operation, when the gradient of adjacent slope of main line is greater than or equal to 1 ‰, vertical curve connection shall be adopted, as shown in Figure 3-6.

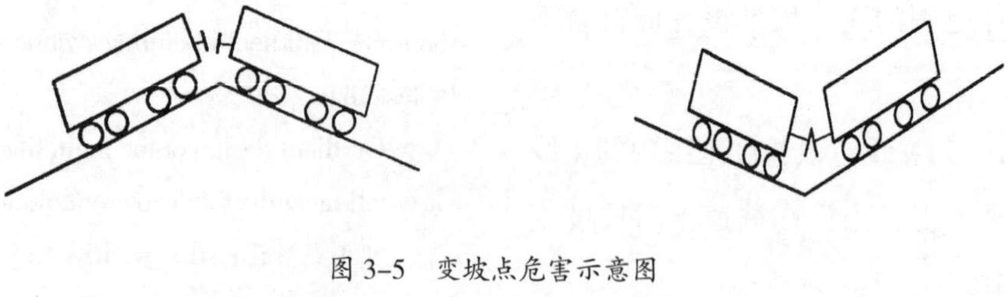

图 3-5　变坡点危害示意图

Figure 3-5　Schematic Figure of Hazards Caused by Point of Gradient Change

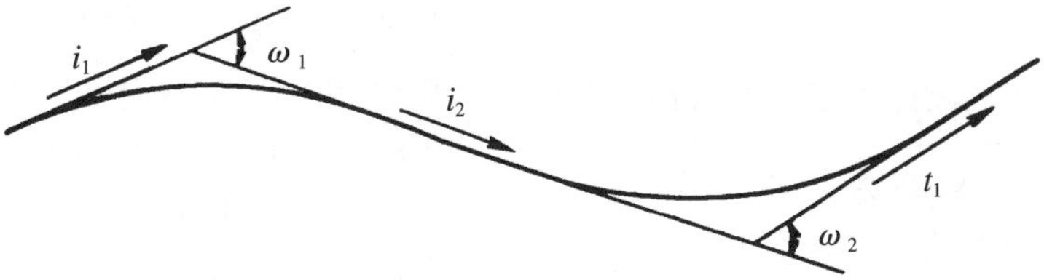

凹形竖曲线 concave vertical curve　凸形竖曲线 convex vertical curve

图 3-6　竖曲线示意图

Figure 3-6　Schematic Diagram of Vertical Curve

竖曲线的线型是圆曲线。有关竖曲线半径的规定如表 3-6、表 3-7 所示。

The line type of vertical curve is circular curve. Radius of vertical curve is specified in Chart 3-6 and Chart 3-7.

表 3-6　最小竖曲线半径

Chart 3-6　Minimum Radius of Vertical Curve

设计速度（千米 / 时）	350	300	250
最小竖曲线半径（米）	25000	25000	20000

设计速度（千米 / 时）design speed（km/h）　最小竖曲线半径（米）minimum radius of vertical curve（m）

表 3-7　限速地段最小竖曲线半径

Chart 3-7　Minimum Radius of Vertical Curve in Limited-Speed Zone

设计速度（千米 / 时）	200	160	120	80
最小竖曲线半径（米）	15000	15000	10000	5000

设计速度（千米 / 时）design speed（km/h）　最小竖曲线半径（米）minimum radius of vertical curve（m）

知识点四：坡段长度

Key Point 4：Length of Grade Section

在列车通过变坡点时会产生附加离心力和附加加速度，为了使行车平稳，宜设计较长的坡段。但为了适应线路高程的变化，坡段也不能太长，否则将造成较大的工程量，给施工带来困难。因此应综合考虑两者的影响来确定最短坡

Additional centrifugal force and acceleration will be generated when train passes through point of gradient change. To keep it running smooth，a longer grade section should be designed. However，the grade section should not be too long due to adaptation of change of route vertical. Otherwise，it

段长度。

（1）正线宜设计为较长的坡段。最小坡段长度在一般条件下不应小于 900 米，困难条件下不应小于 600 米，列车全部停站的车站两端不应小于 400 米。

（2）最小坡段长度不宜连续采用，在困难条件下也不应连续采用。

（3）动车组走行线最小坡段长度不宜小于 200 米，且竖曲线不应重叠。

will cause large quantities of work and bring difficulties to construction. Therefore, both influences should be considered comprehensively to determine the shortest length of grade section.

（1）Long grade section should be designed in main line. The minimum length of grade section shall not be less than 900m under general condition and 600m under difficult condition. Both ends of station for all trains parking shall not be less than 400m.

（2）Minimum length of grade section should not be used continuously or under difficult condition.

（3）The minimum length of grade section for EMU running track should not be less than 200m，and vertical curves shall not overlap.

学习笔记
Study Notes

模块三　课堂练习

问题 1：根据所学内容说明高速铁路线路纵断面有哪些要素？

问题 2：高速铁路线路最大（小）坡度的确定要考虑哪些因素？

Module 3　In-class Exercises

Question 1：Summarize the components of line profile for high speed railway according to what you've learned.

Question 2：What factors shall be considered in determining the maximum (minimum) gradient of high speed railway?

课堂练习

In-class Exercises

模块四　课后拓展

查阅和收集高速铁路设计规范和标准，学习和分析线路纵断面设计的相关规定。

Module 4　After-class Activity

Consult and collect design codes and standards of high speed railway. Learn and analyze the relevant provisions of line profile design.

课后拓展

After-class Activity

项目四　高速铁路线路及道岔

Project 4　Line and Turnout of High Speed Railway

任务一　线路基本构成及其分类

Task 1　Basic Composition and Classification of Line

模块一　学前准备

你见过高铁线路吗？请你通过网络搜索 1~2 幅高铁线路的实物照片，并打印、粘贴在下方，同时写出你看到了什么。

Module 1　Preparation before Class

Have you ever seen a high speed railway line? Please search online for 1~2 pictures of high speed railway line，print and paste them below. Write down what you see.

课前学习笔记
Study Notes before Class

模块二 课堂学习

Module 2 In-class Learning

知识点一：线路的定义

Key Point 1：Definition of Line

线路是指为容许列车以超过时速200千米运营特地兴建或改建的铁路线，是保证高速铁路列车能有走行速度快、安全可靠及乘坐舒适性良好的轨道的整体工程结构。

Line refers to a railway line specially built or rebuilt to allow trains to exceed 200 kilometers per hour. It is an overall engineering structure to ensure high speed railway train fast running speed，reliable safety and good riding comfort.

图 4–1 高速铁路线路

Figure 4–1 High Speed Railway Line

知识点二：线路基本构成

Key Point 2：Basic Composition of Line

在路基、桥隧建筑物修成之后，就可在其上铺设轨道。轨道由钢轨、轨枕、道床、扣件、防爬设备及道岔等主要部件组成。

After earthworks，bridges and tunnels are completed，tracks can be laid on them. Tracks is composed of steel rails，sleepers，track beds，fastenings，anti-creeping device，and turnouts，etc.

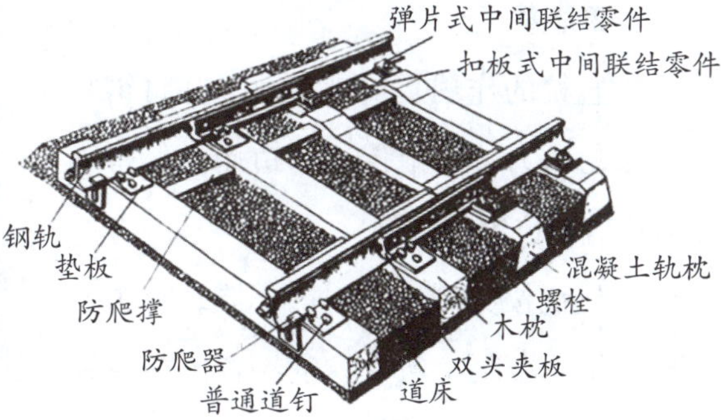

钢轨 steel rail　垫板 pad　防爬撑 anti-creep strut　防爬器 anti-creeper　普通道钉 common track spike
道床 track bed　双头夹板 joint bar　木枕 wooden sleeper　螺栓 bolt　混凝土轨枕 concrete sleeper
扣板式中间联结零件 clamp fastening joint accessory　弹片式中间联结零件 elastic clip joint accessory

图 4-2　轨道

Figure 4-2　Track

1. 钢轨

钢轨的作用是引导车轮的运行方向，直接承受车轮的巨大作用力并将其传递给轨枕。在电气化铁路和自动闭塞区段，钢轨作为轨道电路使用。

钢轨的断面形状采用具有最佳抗弯性能的工字形断面，由轨头、轨腰、轨底三部分组成。

1. Steel Rail

The role of steel rail is to guide the running direction of wheels. Rails directly bear the huge force of wheels and transfer it to sleepers. Rails are used as track circuit in electrified railway and automatic block section.

The sectional shape of steel rail adopts an I-shaped section with the best bending resistance performance, which is composed of rail head, rail web and rail base.

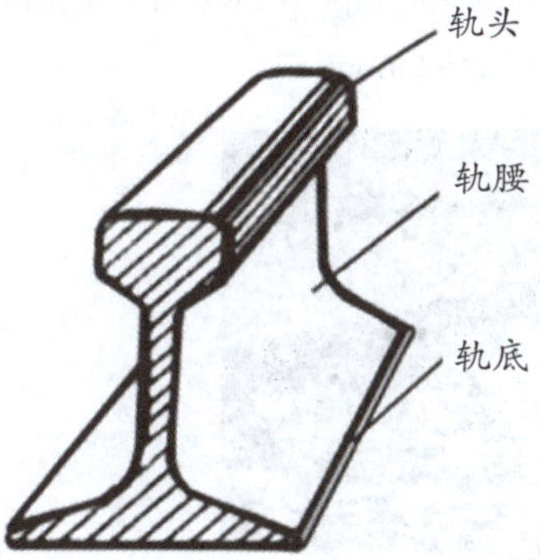

轨头 rail head　轨腰 rail web　轨底 rail base

图 4-3　钢轨断面

Figure 4-3　Rail Section

2. 轨枕

轨枕的作用是支承钢轨，并将钢轨传来的压力均匀地传递给道床，保持钢轨应有的位置和轨距。

轨枕按其制作材料的不同，分为木枕、钢筋混凝土轨枕。世界各国高速铁路有砟轨道均采用钢筋混凝土轨枕。

2. Sleeper

The function of sleeper is to support steel rail and evenly transfer pressure from steel rail to track bed, maintaining the proper position and track gauge.

Sleepers include wooden sleeper and reinforced concrete sleeper according to its different materials. Concrete sleepers are commonly used in high speed ballasted railway tracks all over the world.

图 4-4　钢筋混凝土轨枕

Figure 4-4　Reinforced Concrete Sleeper

3. 道床

高速铁路线路的道床有足够的厚度，以减少路基面所受的压力和振动，保证路基顶面不发生永久性变形。

3. Track Bed

Track bed of high speed railway lines has sufficient thickness to reduce pressure and vibration on track formation. Meanwhile, it prevents the top surface of earthwork from permanent deformation.

图 4-5　道床

Figure 4-5　Track Bed

4. 扣件

由于高速铁路列车运行速度高，要求扣件的弹性件具有：足够的扣压力，相当的弹程，保持轨距的很强的能力，足够的强度和耐久性，良好的降噪、减震性能，及良好的绝缘性能。

扣件因轨枕的不同，分为木枕扣件和钢筋混凝土轨枕扣件两类。高速铁路常用钢筋混凝土轨枕扣件。

4. Fastening

Due to fast running speed of high speed train, the elastic parts of fastenings shall include following features: sufficient clamping force, equivalent elastic range, strong ability to maintain track gauge, sufficient strength and durability, good noise and vibration reduction, and good insulation property.

Fastenings include wooden sleeper fastening and reinforced concrete sleeper fastening based on different sleepers. Reinforced concrete fastenings are commonly used in high speed railway.

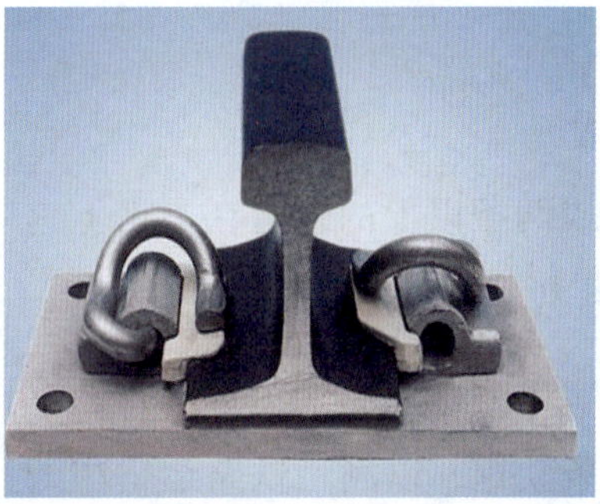

图 4–6 钢筋混凝土轨枕扣件

Figure 4–6 Reinforced Concrete Sleeper Fastening

5. 防爬设备

在列车运行所产生的纵向力的作用下，钢轨会产生纵向移动，有时还会带动轨枕一起移动，这种现象叫作轨道爬行。

轨道爬行往往引起轨缝不匀、轨枕歪斜等线路病害，对轨道的破坏性极大，严重时还会危及行车安全。因此，必须采用有效措施加以防止，如设置防爬器与防爬撑。常用的防爬器为穿销式防爬器。

5. Anti–Creeping Device

Under the action of the longitudinal force generated by train operation, rails will move longitudinally, sometimes driving sleepers to move together with it, and this phenomenon is called track creeping.

Track creeping often causes problems as uneven rail joint gap, skewed sleepers, etc. which are extremely destructive to tracks and even endanger running safety in severe cases. Therefore, effective measures must be taken to prevent it, such as installing anti–creeper and anti–creep strut. The commonly used anti–creeper is wedged rail anchor.

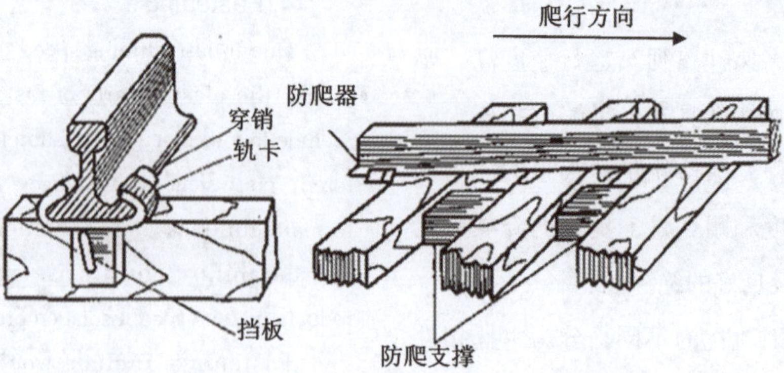

穿销 wedge　轨卡 rail clip　挡板 obstacle board　防爬器 anti-creeper
防爬支撑 anti-creep strut　爬行方向 creeping direction

图 4-7　穿销式防爬器
Figure 4-7　Wedged Rail Anchor

6. 道岔

两条或两条以上的轨道在平面上进行相互连接或交叉的设备，被称为道岔。其作用是使机车车辆由一条轨道转入或越过另一条轨道，以满足铁路运输中的各种作业需要。详细介绍见项目四的任务二。

6. Turnout

A device that connects or intersects two or more tracks on a plane is called turnout. Its function is to make locomotives run from one track to another or pass over another track to meet various operational needs in railway transportation. For details, see Task 2 in Project 4.

图 4-8　高铁道岔
Figure 4-8　High Speed Railway Turnout

7. 车挡

设置在尽头线末端，用于阻止由于操作不当而使机车车辆冲出尽头线或撞坏其他构筑物。

7. Bumper Post

Bumper post is set at the end of stub-end siding and used for preventing locomotives from rushing out of stub-end siding or damaging other structures due to improper operation.

图 4-9　高铁车挡

Figure 4-9　High Speed Railway Bumper Post

学习笔记

Study Notes

模块三　课堂练习

Module 3　In-class Exercises

问题 1：根据所学知识，圈出并标明图 4-10 中出现的轨道结构的详细名称。

Question 1：Please circle and mark the detailed names of track structure in Figure 4-10 according to what you've learned.

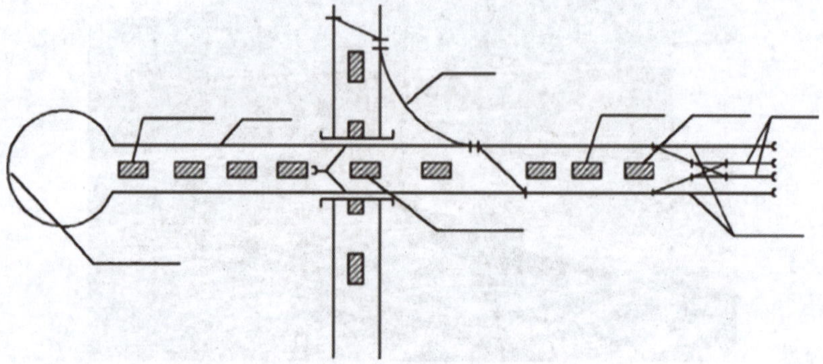

图 4-10　轨道结构

Figure 4-10　Structure of Track

问题 2：请在图 4-11 中正确标出不同线路类型的名称。

Question 2：Please mark the names of different lines correctly in Figure 4-11.

图 4-11　不同类型线路

Figure 4-11　Different Classification of Line

课堂练习

In-class Exercises

模块四　课后拓展

什么是有砟轨道，什么是无砟轨道？请你查询网络资料，找到有砟轨道和无砟轨道的照片，打印并粘贴在下框内，同时进行简单的文字介绍。

Module 4　After-class Activity

What is a ballasted track? What is a ballastless track? Please search online and find photos of ballasted track and ballastless track. Print and paste the photos below and write down a brief introduction.

课后拓展

After-class Activity

任务二　道岔基本构成及其分类

Task 2　Basic Composition and Classification of Turnout

模块一　学前准备

你见过高铁道岔吗？请你通过网络搜索 1~2 幅高铁道岔的实物照片，打印并粘贴在下方，同时请你写出这种设备的作用是什么。

Module 1　Preparation before Class

Have you ever seen high speed railway turnouts? Please search online for 1~2 pictures of the high speed railway turnouts, print and paste them below. Think and write down the function of this equipment.

课前学习笔记
Study Notes before Class

模块二　课堂学习

Module 2　In-class Learning

知识点一：道岔的定义

Key Point 1：Definition of Turnout

机车车辆在运行过程中，常常需要由一条线路转入另一条线路，或跨越其他线路。这就需要设置线路的连接与交叉设备，即道岔。

道岔是铁路轨道的重要组成部分。由于道岔数量多、使用寿命短、限制列车速度、行车安全性低，其与曲线、接头并称轨道的三大薄弱环节。

Locomotives often transfer or pass over from one track to another. It is necessary to set up connecting and crossing equipment on tracks，and that is turnout.

Turnout is an important part of railway tracks. Due to its large numbers，short service life，limited train speed and low running safety，they are called the three weaknesses of tracks together with curves and joints.

图 4–12　道岔实物图（单开道岔）

Figure 4–12　Turnout（Single Turnout）

知识点二：道岔的分类

Key Point 2：Classification of Turnout

1. 单开道岔

单开道岔是最简单、最常用的一种道岔，其数量占中国铁路各类道岔总数的 90% 以上。

1. Single Turnout

Single turnout is the simplest and most commonly used，accounting for more than 90% of all turnout types in China's railways.

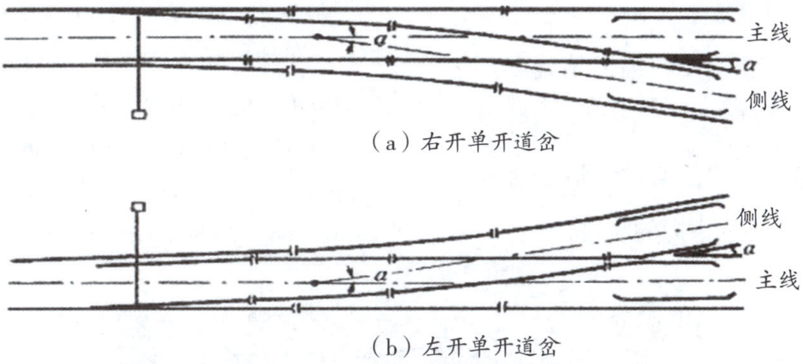

主线 main line　侧线 side line　右开单开道岔 right-hand single turnout
左开单开道岔 left-hand single turnout

图 4-13　单开道岔
Figure 4-13　Single Turnout

2. 对称道岔（双开道岔）

对称道岔是中国煤矿窄轨铁路道岔的一种类型，是窄轨道铁路线路连接的基本设备。

2. Symmetrical Turnout (Double Turnouts)

Symmetrical turnout is a kind of narrow-gauge railway turnout in China's coal mine region. It is the basic equipment for connecting narrow-gauge railway lines.

图 4-14　对称道岔
Figure 4-14　Symmetrical Turnout

3. 三开道岔

三开道岔主要在编组站铺设。它是将一个道岔纳入另一个道岔内构成的一种特殊道岔型式，通过一组道岔可以实现开通 3 个不同方向的线路。

3. Three-Way Turnouts

Three-way turnouts are mainly laid in marshalling station. It is a special turnout formed by bringing one turnout into another. Three lines can be opened in different directions by a group of turnouts.

图 4-15　三开道岔

Figure 4-15　Three-Way Turnout

知识点三：单开道岔的基本构成

单开道岔由三大基本部分构成：转辙器部分、连接部分、辙叉及护轨部分。详细构成见图 4-16、图 4-17。

Key Point 3：Basic Composition of Single Turnout

Single turnout consists of three basic parts：switch part，connecting part，frog and guard rail. For detailed structure，see Figure 4-16 and Figure 4-17.

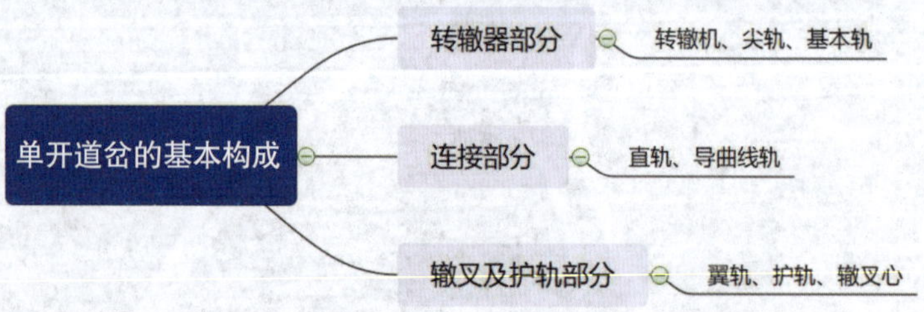

单开道岔的基本构成 composition of single turnout　转辙器部分 switch part　转辙机 switch machine　尖轨 switch rail　基本轨 stock rail　连接部分 connecting part　直轨 straight rail　导曲线轨 lead curve rail　辙叉及护轨部分 frog and guard rail　翼轨 wing rail　护轨 guard rail　辙叉心 point of frog

图 4-16　单开道岔的基本构成

Figure 4-16　Basic Composition of Single Turnout

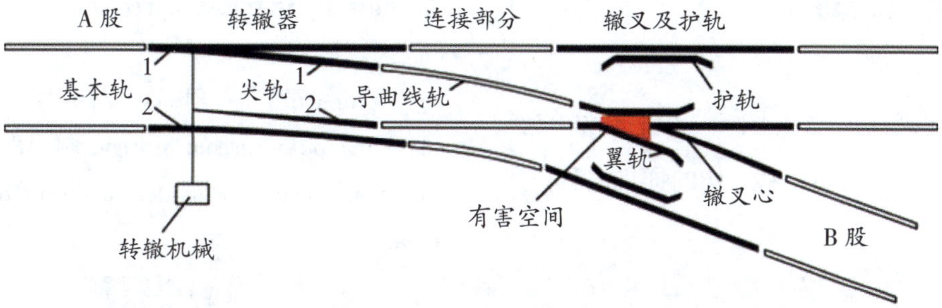

A 股 Track A　转辙器 switch machine　连接部分 connecting part　辙叉及护轨 frog and guard rail
基本轨 stock rail　尖轨 switch rail　导曲线轨 lead curve rail　护轨 guard rail　翼轨 wing rail
辙叉心 point of frog　B 股 Track B　转辙机械 switching device　有害空间 gap in the frog

图 4–17　单开道岔基本构成示意图

Figure 4–17　Schematic Figure of Basic Composition of Single Turnout

学习笔记
Study Notes

模块三 课堂练习

Module 3 In-class Exercises

问题 1：写出图 4-18 中道岔的类型，圈出并标明道岔结构的详细名称。

Question 1: Please write down the classification of turnout in Figure 4-18. Circle and mark structure names of the turnout in detail.

图 4-18 道岔结构

Figure 4-18 Structure of Turnout

问题 2：请你在下框里绘制单开道岔的示意图，并标出各个部分的详细名称。

Question 2: Please draw a schematic diagram of single turnout in the box below and mark names of each part in detail.

课堂练习

In-class Exercises

模块四　课后拓展

在单开道岔的类型中，左开单开道岔和右开单开道岔分别是什么样的？请你查询网络资料，分别找到左开单开道岔和右开单开道岔的照片，打印并粘贴在下框内，同时进行简要的文字说明。

Module 4　After-class Activity

What is left-hand single turnout? What is right-hand single turnout? Please search online and find photos of those two turnouts respectively. Print and paste the photos in the box below and write down a brief introduction.

课后拓展

After-class Activity

项目五　高速铁路车站分布及车站设计

Project 5　Distribution and Design of High Speed Railway Station

任务一　高速铁路车站的分布

Task 1　Distribution of High Speed Railway Station

模块一　学前准备

Module 1　Preparation before Class

查阅资料，说明高速铁路车站都有哪些类型。

Do research and explain the types of high speed railway station.

课前学习笔记

Study Notes before Class

模块二　课堂学习

Module 2　In-class Learning

知识点一：高速铁路车站类型

Key Point 1：Types of High Speed Railway Station

图 5-1　高速铁路车站

Figure 5-1　High Speed Railway Station

高速铁路车站主要是为高速客流提供运输服务的，其服务对象决定了车站在功能和分类上有别于普通的铁路车站。

High speed railway stations mainly provide transportation service for high speed passenger flow, and the service targets determine that high speed railway stations are different from ordinary railway stations in function and classification.

按车站的作业性质及其在线路上的位置将高速铁路车站分为越行站、中间站和始发站三类。根据客运量的大小将车站分为大、中、小型车站。一般情况下，直辖市、省会城市所在地的车站为大型站，省辖市所在地的车站为中型站，县城、县级市的车站为小型站。

According to the nature of station operation and their location on line, high speed stations are divided into three types: overtaking station, intermediate station and departure station. Stations are also divided into large station, medium station and small station by passenger traffic volume. In general, stations locating at municipalities and provincial capital cities are large stations. Stations locating at provincial cities are medium stations. Stations in county and county-level cities are small stations.

高速铁路车站 high speed railway station　中间站 intermediate station　越行站 overtaking station　始发、终到站 departure station　枢纽站 junction station

图 5-2　高速铁路车站的分类

Figure 5-2　Types of High Speed Railway Station

按照作业性质及在线路上的位置进行分类，中间站的范围相当广泛，不但包括了沿线市、县所有车站，也包括了直辖市和省会的车站。另外，中间站的规模差别也非常大。具有 2 ~ 11 个站台面的车站均属中间站，由于名称体现不了它的特性，增加了一类“枢纽站”。因此，高速铁路车站被分为越行站、中间站、始发站和枢纽站四类车站。

According to the nature of station operation and their location on line, the scale of intermediate stations is quite extensive, not only including stations in cities and counties along the line, but also including stations in municipalities and provincial capital cities. In addition, the scale of intermediate stations is also quite different. Stations with 2~11 platforms are intermediate stations. Because the name does not reflect its characteristics, a type of "junction station" has been added. Therefore, they are totally divided into four types: overtaking station, intermediate station, departure station and junction station.

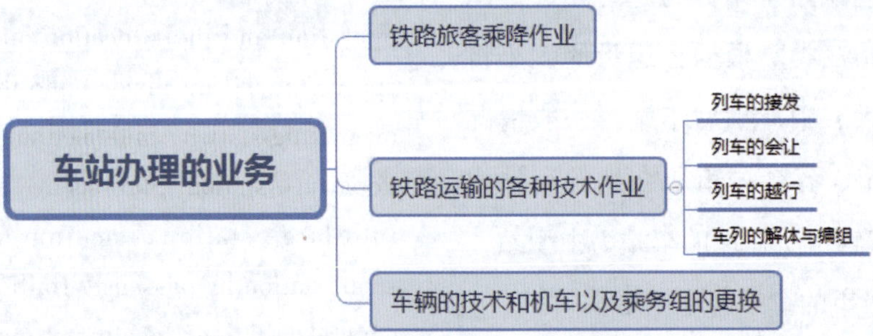

车站办理的业务 station service　铁路旅客乘降作业 railway passengers on and off　铁路运输的各种技术作业 various technical operations of railway transportation　列车的接发 train arrival / departure　列车的会让 train passing / crossing　列车的越行 train overtaking　车列的解体与编组 train break-up and marshalling　车辆的技术和机车以及乘务组的更换 vehicle technology and locomotive / crew shift

图 5-3　车站办理的业务

Figure 5-3　Station Service

高速铁路的车站是高速铁路枢纽系统的核心，是铁路运输的关键节点，是办理客货运输组织的基地，也是铁路系统的一个基本生产单位。

High speed railway station is the core of high speed railway terminal system, the key joint of railway transportation, the base for handling passenger and freight transportation, and a basic production unit of railway system.

知识点二：中间站站坪长度

Key Point 2：Length of Intermediate Station Site

在铁路正线的平面和纵断面上设置车站配线的地段叫作站坪。车站两端正线最外方道岔基本轨始端（警冲标）之间的距离为站坪长度。

The section where station wiring is set up on the plane and profile of main line is called a station site. The distance between stock rails at both ends of station （fouling post） is the length of station site.

影响站坪长度的因素 factors affecting length of station site　道岔区长度 length of turnout section
到发线有效长 effective length of receiving–departure track
远期车站布置图形（岛式或侧式）long–term station layout （island / side）
到发线数量 number of arrival–departure track

图 5–4　影响站坪长度的因素
Figure 5–4　Factors Affecting Length of Station Site

具体站坪长度见表 5–1。

The specific length of station site is shown in the Chart 5–1.

表 5–1　站坪长度
Chart 5–1　Station Site

路段设计行车速度（千米 / 时）	远期到发线有效长度（米）				
	布置图类型	700		450	
		有渡线	无渡线	有渡线	无渡线
200 ~ 250	侧式	1450	1700	1250	1500
	岛式	1600	2000	1400	1800
300 ~ 350	侧式	2000	2500	1800	2300
	岛式	3500	4000	3100	3600

路段设计行车速度（千米/时）design running speed of railway section（km/h）
远期到发线有效长度（米）long-term effective length of receiving-departure track（m）
布置图类型 type of layout　有渡线 crossover　无渡线 non-crossover　侧式 side　岛式 island

知识点三：高速铁路车站分布原则　Key Point 3：Principles of High Speed Station Distribution

1. 车站分布考虑的因素　1. Essentials for Station Distribution

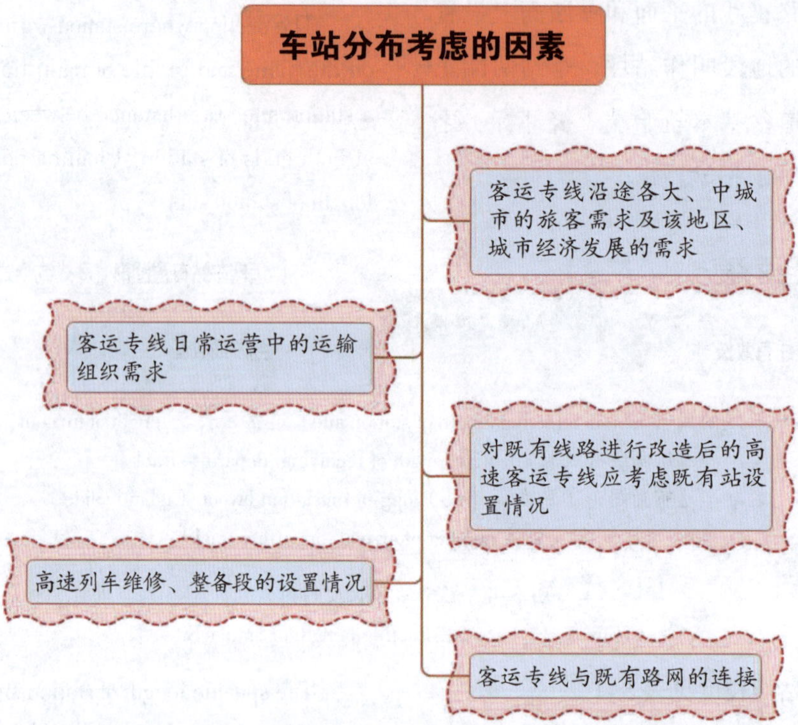

车站分布考虑的因素 essentials for station distribution
客运专线沿途各大、中城市的旅客需求及该地区、城市经济发展的需求 requirements of passengers from cities along the line and that of local area and its economic development
客运专线日常运营中的运输组织需求 requirements of daily operational transport organization
对既有线路进行改造后的高速客运专线应考虑既有站设置情况 existing passenger station setting should be considered after reconstructing existing line into high speed passenger dedicated line
高速列车维修、整备段的设置情况 maintenance and servicing depot conditions for high speed train
客运专线与既有路网的连接 connection between passenger dedicated line and existing railway network

图 5-5　车站分布考虑的因素
Figure 5-5　Essentials for Station Distribution

2. 国外高速铁路车站布置情况

2. Setting of Foreign High Speed Railway Station

表 5-2　国外高速铁路车站分布情况

Chart 5-2　Setting of Foreign High Speed Railway Stations

国别	线路别	线路长度 / km	车站数量	站间距离 /km			线路使用方式
				平均	最长	最短	
日本	东海道线	515.4	15	36.8	68.1	15.9	客运专线
	山阳线	553.7	18	32.6	55.9	10.5	客运专线
	东北线	496.5	18	29.2	48.9	3.6	客运专线
	上越线	269.5	9	33.7	41.8	23.6	客运专线
	北陆线	117.4	6	23.5	33.2	17.6	客运专线
法国	东南线	426	4	142.0	305	50	客运专线
	大西洋线	281	4	93.7	168	59	客运专线
	北方线	326	4	108.7	127	99	客运专线
	东南延伸线	121	2	121	121	121	客运专线
	地中海线	223	4	74.3	129	12	客运专线
德国	汉诺威—维尔茨堡	327	5	81.8	—	—	客运混跑
	曼海姆—斯图加特	105	2	105	105	—	客运混跑
	汉诺威—柏林	264	5	66.0	130	10	客运混跑
	科隆—法兰克福	202	4	67.3	—	—	客运专线
意大利	罗马—佛罗伦萨	237	19	13.2	—	—	客运混跑
西班牙	马德里—塞维利亚	471	4	157.0	—	—	客运混跑
韩国	首尔—釜山	430	6	86.0	126.8	62.9	客运专线

国别 country　日本 Japan　法国 France　德国 Germany　意大利 Italy　西班牙 Spain　韩国 South Korea
线路别 line　东海道线 Tokaido Line　山阳线 Sanyo Line　东北线 Tohoku Line　上越线 Joetsu Line
北陆线 Hokuriku Line　东南线 Southeast Line　大西洋线 TGV Atlantique Line　北方线 North Line
东南延伸线 Southeast Extending Line　地中海线 Mediterranean Line
汉诺威—维尔茨堡 Hanover-Wurzburg　曼海姆—斯图加特 Mannheim-Stuttgart
汉诺威—柏林 Hanover-Berlin　科隆—法兰克福 Koln-Frankfurt　罗马—佛罗伦萨 Rome-Florence
马德里—塞维利亚 Madrid-Seville　首尔—釜山 Seoul-Busan

图 5–6 日本山阳新干线小仓新车站

Figure 5–6 Japanese Sanyo Shinkansen Kokura Station

3. 我国客运专线车站分布原则

3. Principles of Station Distribution for China’s Passenger Dedicated Line

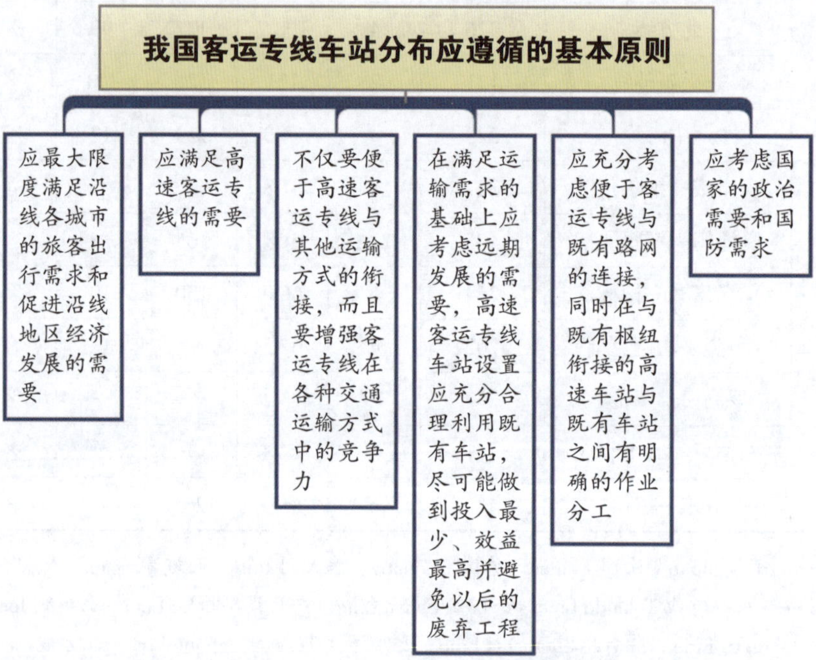

我国客运专线车站分布应遵循的基本原则 basic principles of station distribution for passenger dedicated line in China　应最大限度满足沿线各城市的旅客出行需求和促进沿线地区经济发展的需要 meet passengers’ travel needs in cities along the line and promote economic development of areas along the line to the greatest extent　应满足高速客运专线的需要 meet the needs of high speed passenger dedicated line

不仅要便于高速客运专线与其他运输方式的衔接，而且要增强客运专线在各种交通运输方式中的竞争力 facilitate connections between high speed passenger dedicated line and other modes of transportation, enhance the competitiveness of passenger dedicated line in various modes of transportation

在满足运输需求的基础上应考虑远期发展的需要，高速客运专线车站设置应充分合理利用既有车站，尽可能做到投入最少、效益最高并避免以后的废弃工程 on the basis of meeting transportation needs, long-term development needs shall be considered, station setting of high speed passenger dedicated line shall make fully reasonable use of existing station, try to gain the highest benefit with the least investment and avoid future abandonment of projects　应充分考虑便于客运专线与既有路网的连接，同时在与既有枢纽衔接的高速车站与既有车站之间有明确的作业分工 full consideration shall be given to the connection between passenger dedicated line and existing railway network，there should be a clear work division between high speed station connected with existing junction station and existing station　应考虑国家的政治需要和国防需求 national political and defense needs shall be taken into account

图 5-7　我国客运专线车站分布应遵循的基本原则

Figure 5-7　Basic Principles of Station Distribution for Passenger Dedicated Line in China

在一般情况下，包括越行站在内的平均站间距离以 30~50 千米为宜。当自然分布的客运站距离大于 50 千米，且该区间通过能力不受限制时，其间可不加越行站，也可预留远期加站条件。

合理距离设置的作用是保证旅客列车在路段内的平均运行速度达到一定的值，从而有效缩短旅客在途时间，提高机车车辆运用指标。该值约为路段设计最高行车速度的 0.75 ~ 0.85。根据上述基础计算，合理的路段最小长度约为加减速距离之和的 2.5 倍。故路段最小长度可据此条件计算。

Generally，the average distance between two stations，including an overtaking station is preferably 30~50 km. When the distance between naturally distributed passenger stations is longer than 50 km and carrying capacity is not limited in the section，there is no need to set an overtaking station and it's better to reserve long-term conditions for adding future station.

Reasonable distance is to ensure that the average running speed of passenger trains in railway section reaches a certain value，so as to shorten passengers traveling time effectively and improve locomotives' application index. The value is about 0.75 ~ 0.85 of the highest design running speed of railway. According to the basic calculation above，the reasonable minimum length of railway section is about 2.5 times of the sum of acceleration and deceleration distance. Therefore，the minimum length of railwaysection can be calculated by this condition.

图 5-8　武汉高铁车站

Figure 5-8　Wuhan High Speed Railway Station

学习笔记

Study Notes

模块三　课堂练习

问题 1：根据已学知识归纳、总结高速铁路车站的类型。

问题 2：讨论高速铁路车站中间站站坪长度如何确定。

问题 3：讨论高速铁路车站的分布原则有哪些。

Module 3　In-class Exercises

Question 1：Summarize the types of high speed railway station according to what you've learned.

Question 2：Discuss how to determine the length of intermediate station site of high speed railway station.

Question 3：Discuss the principles of high speed railway station distribution.

课堂练习
In-class Exercises

模块四　课后拓展

收集附近的高速铁路车站的照片，并根据所学知识分析其类型和业务办理的特点。

Module 4　After-class Activity

Collect photos of nearby high speed railway station and analyze its type and service feature according to what you've learned.

课后拓展

After-class Activity

任务二　高速铁路车站设计特点及主要内容

Task 2　Design Features and Main Content for High Speed Railway Station

模块一　学前准备

随手拍几张高速铁路车站的照片，试说明高速铁路车站的设计特点。

Module 1　Preparation before Class

Take a few photos of a high speed railway station and try to explain its design feature.

课前学习笔记
Study Notes before Class

模块二　课堂学习

知识点一：高速铁路车站设计特点

1. 车站作业单一，只办客运业务，不办货运业务

考虑到以下几个因素，高速铁路车站更适宜于只办客运业务。

货车轴重：货车轴重大多在 21 吨以上，而高速铁路上的货车轴重不宜超过 18 吨。

速度差：客货运列车速度差较大，共线运行必将降低旅客列车速度，成为不合理的运输组织。

信号适应：高速客运铁路行车依靠 ATC 和 CTC，无地面信号，必须采用特制的货运机车和车辆。

必须减少牵引质量，加大牵引功率和减缓最大坡度：货运列车牵引质量在 1000 吨左右，最大坡度不宜超过 12‰，机车功率须加大至 8800kW 左右。

货物列车编组和货物装卸：货物列车编组和货物装卸适用于高附加值的轻快货物列车。列车货源分散，必须在编组站集结。修建通路和配套设施较为困难。

Module 2　In-class Learning

Key Point 1: Design Feature of High Speed Railway Station

1. Single Station Operation: Only Passenger Service is Available, and No Freight Service

Considering the following factors, high speed railway stations are more suitable for only passenger transportation.

Freight car axle load: most of freight car axle load is more than 21t, while the freight car axle load on high speed railway should not exceed 18t.

Speed difference: the speed difference between passenger train and freight train is large, and co-linear operation will definitely reduce the passenger train speed, then it will become an unreasonable transportation organization.

Signal adaptation: high speed passenger railways depend on ATC and CTC, without trackside signal. Special freight locomotive and vehicle must be used.

Reduce tractive tonnage, increase traction power and slow down maximum gradient: the tractive tonnage of freight train is about 1000t, the maximum gradient should not exceed 12‰ and the locomotive power should be increased to about 8800kW.

Freight train marshalling and cargo handling: freight train marshalling and cargo handling are suitable for light freight train with high added-value. Decentralized transport supplies must be assembled at marshalling station. It is difficult to build access roads and supporting facilities.

2. 必须突出“安全第一”的设计思想

高速铁路车站设计必须突出“安全第一”的设计思想，要充分体现出“以人为本，方便旅客”的宗旨，提倡旅客流程立体化、进出站自由化和多样化的设计。高速铁路车站需考虑总体布局，方便旅客进出站和上下车，并做好与其他交通方式的协调。

3. 高速旅客列车不办理行包和邮件装卸业务

为减少工程投资，节约运输成本，减少客运列车停站时间，我国高速铁路车站不应办理行包和邮件装卸作业。

4. 要充分体现“以人为本，方便旅客”的宗旨

在总体布局上，把方便旅客贯穿于城市交通→进出站→上下车整个流程。高速列车间隔时间短，到发站客流量大，设计中应避免交叉干扰，保证安全。应具有旅客流程立体化、进出站自由化、进站口和出站口多样化的现代化设计。

5. 高速铁路车站的客运和行车工作组织、客运设施要适应高效率、快速作业的要求

为适应高速列车在站高效、快速的作业要求，必须改进车站客运组织工作和行车组织工作，并配以先进设备。

2. Design Idea：Security First

High speed railway station must highlight the design idea of “security first”, fully embody the purpose of “people-oriented, passenger convenience”, and advocate three-dimensional passenger service, liberalization of station entry and exit, and diversified design. The overall layout of high speed railway station should be considered to facilitate passengers to enter and exit station, get on and off train, and coordinate with other modes of transportation.

3. Do not Handle Parcel and Mail Operation for High Speed Passenger Train

To decrease project investment, transportation cost and dwell time of passenger train. China's high speed station shall not handle parcel and mail operation.

4. Fully Embody the Purpose of “People-Oriented, Passengers-Convenience”

In terms of general layout, passenger convenience shall run through city transportation, entering and exiting station, getting on and off train. Due to the short interval between high speed trains and large passenger flow at arrival-departure station, cross interference shall be avoided in design to ensure safety. It shall be a modern design with three-dimensional passenger service, freedom of station entry and exit, diversified modern design of entrance and exit.

5. The Organization of Passenger Transportation, Train Operation and Facilities of High Speed Railway Station shall Meet the Requirements of High Efficiency and Fast Operation

To meet the requirements of efficient and fast operation of high speed train at station, it is necessary to improve the organization of passenger transportation and train operation at station, and equip it with advanced equipment.

图 5–9　车站设备

Figure 5–9　Station Equipment

（1）客运组织。

应该设置进站至站台全程醒目、清晰的旅客引导电子设备和多处一定时间段内各次列车电子信息牌；每个旅客能方便地“对门上车、对号入座”；根据客运量配备自动售票、自动识别系统。

（2）行车组织。

车站应有自动控制接发列车信号系统，减少办理闭塞和开通进路的时间。在平面设计时保证列车以 80 千米 / 时的

（1）Passenger service organization.

Electronic equipment for guiding passengers and electronic information boards for various trains within a certain period of time shall be set up from entrance to platform. Each passenger can conveniently “board to the right door and sit in the right seat”. Provide an automatic ticketing and identification system based on passenger capacity.

（2）Train operation organization.

Stations shall have automatic control systems for receiving–departure train signals

速度进入进站信号机，能安全、准确到达停车位，保证通过列车不减速通过，确保会车安全。

to reduce time for blocking and clear routes. Layout design shall ensure that trains can enter the home signal at a speed of 80km/h and reach the parking space safely and accurately. It ensures that passing trains do not decelerate, as well as passing safety.

知识点二：高速铁路车站设计的主要内容

Key Point 2：Main Content of High Speed Railway Station Design

高速铁路车站设计应包括以下主要内容：方案比选、总图及平面布置、纵横断面、一般路基土石方、排水、用地和工程数量计算等工作。

（1）高速车站平面和纵断面设计：越行站、中间站、枢纽站、始发终到站。

（2）区间渡线。

（3）高中速联络线。

（4）疏解区：包括高速线与高速线、高速线与普速线。

（5）走行线：包括各种段、所、区等与高速站（或高速正线）间的各种走行线。

（6）各类段、所、区的线路及股道布置：高速动车检修段、高速动车运用所、高速动车折返所、中速机车整备所、中速机车检修段、工务段、供电段等。

High speed station shall carry out the following main contents：scheme comparison，general layout，plan layout，plane/profile，general earthwork and stonework，drainage，land use and engineering quantity calculation，etc.

（1）Horizontal and vertical section design of high speed station：overtaking station，intermediate station，junction station，departure and arrival station.

（2）Section crossover.

（3）High and medium speed connecting line.

（4）Untwining area includes high speed railway and high speed railway，high speed railway and normal speed railway.

（5）Running tracks include various running tracks between various depot，workshop，section，etc. and high speed station（or high speed main line）.

（6）Layout of tracks and lines of various depot，workshop and section：high speed EMU maintenance depot，high speed EMU workshop，high speed EMU turnaround workshop，medium speed locomotive servicing depot，medium speed maintenance depot，track division，power supply division，etc.

图 5-10 站场

Figure 5-10 Station and Yard

知识点三：高速铁路车站建设原则

1. 功能性

铁路客运站功能性的核心内涵就是“以人为本、以流为主”。

（1）注重流线组织，缩小换乘距离。

流线组织简洁顺畅。

流线组织短捷合理。

站内导向直观明确。

（2）为旅客提供舒适的站内空间。

（3）为旅客提供良好的站内服务。

舒适的候车服务。

便捷的乘降服务。

方便的信息服务。

周到的商业服务。

Key Point 3: Principles of High Speed Station Construction

1. Functional Nature

The core of railway station functionality is “people-oriented and flow-oriented”.

(1) Emphasis on flow line organization and reduce transfer distance.

Simple and smooth flow line organization.

Short and reasonable flow line organization.

Visual and clear in-station guidance.

(2) Provide comfortable in-station space for passengers.

(3) Provide good in-station service for passengers.

Comfortable waiting service.

Convenient passenger on and off service.

Convenient information service.

Considerate business service.

图 5-11　超大跨度空间钢结构技术

Figure 5-11　Super Long Span Space Steel Structure Technology

2. 系统性

按照“系统集成、整体最优”的原则，以客运站为中心，实现城市其他交通工具与铁路之间的有机结合、系统优化，建立可供各种交通方式换乘的综合枢纽。

（1）与城市规划相协调。

站址选择应与城市规划相配合。

铁路客运站应与城市融为一体。

客运站应与城市轨道交通、道路交通有效衔接。

2. Systematic Nature

According to the principle of “system integration and overall optimization”, it shall take passenger station as the center, realize the organic combination and system optimization between other urban transportation means and railways, and establish a comprehensive hub for various modes of transportation transfer.

(1) Coordinate with city overall planning.

Site selection shall be coordinated with city overall planning.

Railway passenger station shall be integrated with cities.

Passenger station shall be effectively connected with urban rail transit and road traffic.

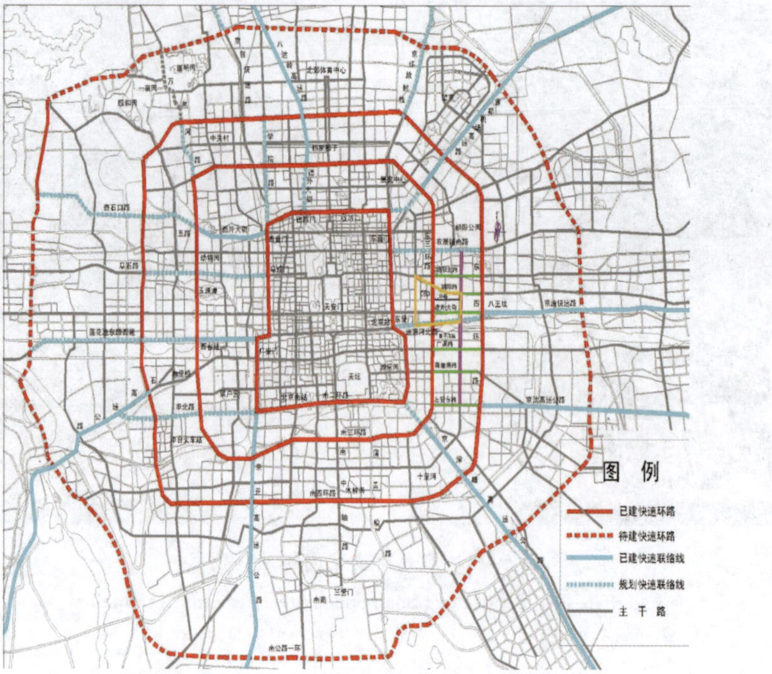

图 5-12　以客运站为中心的综合枢纽

Figure 5-12　Comprehensive Hub Centered on Passengers Station

（2）客运站各组成部分形成统一整体。

（3）铁路客运站专业系统应实现整体最优。

（2）Each component of the passenger station forms a unified whole.

（3）Professional system of railway passenger station shall realize overall optimization.

3. 先进性

（1）前瞻性的规模、布局与标准。

（2）完善的公共安全技术。

结构安全。

消防安全。

交通疏解安全。

（3）先进的节能环保技术。

节能降耗。

减振降噪。

3. Advanced Nature

（1）Prospective scale，layout and standard.

（2）Complete public safety technology.

structural safety.

fire control safety.

traffic relief safety.

（3）Advanced energy-saving and environmental protection technology.

saving energy and reducing consumption.

reducing vibration and noise.

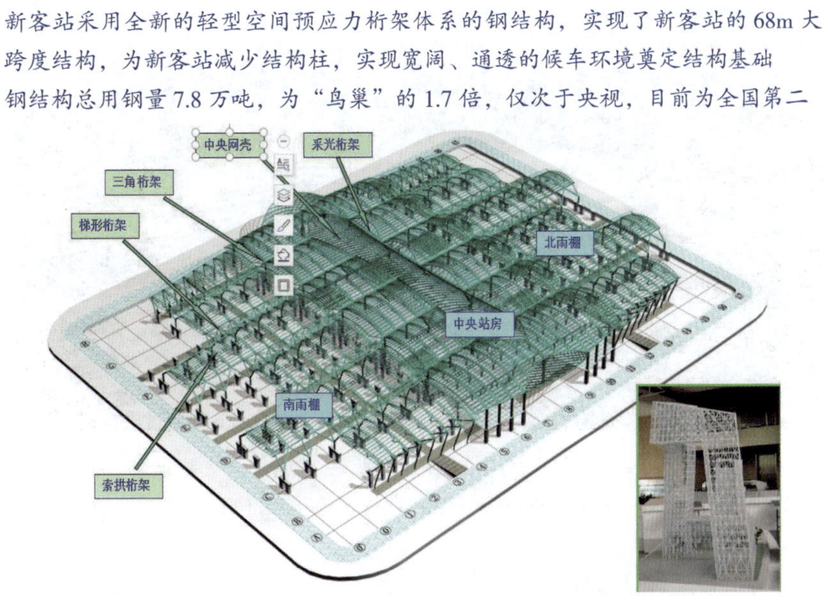

新客站采用全新的轻型空间预应力桁架体系的钢结构，实现了新客站的68m大跨度结构，为新客站减少结构柱，实现宽阔、通透的候车环境奠定结构基础 the new station adopts a new steel structure of light space pre-stressed truss system, it realizes the 68m long-span structure and lays a structural foundation for the new station to reduce its structural column，and create a broad and bright waiting environment
钢结构总用钢量7.8万吨，为“鸟巢”的1.7倍，仅次于央视，目前为全国第二 the total steel consumption is 78000 tons，which is 1.7 times of that used in the Bird's Nest Stadium，ranking only second to the CCTV Tower and currently the second in China

梯形桁架 trapezoid truss　三角桁架 triangle truss　中央网壳 the central latticed shell
采光桁架 daylighting truss　北雨棚 north canopy　中央站房 the central station building
南雨棚 south canopy　索拱桁架 cable arch truss

图 5-13　新客运站结构

Figure 5-13　Structure of New Passenger Station

4. 文化性

（1）体现地域特征及人文特征。

地域特征。

人文特征。

（2）体现时代特征。

（3）体现交通建筑特征。

体现交通功能的空间特点。

体现简约的建筑风格。

4. Cultural Nature

（1）Reflect regional and humanistic characteristic.

Regional characteristic.

Humanistic characteristic.

（2）Reflect characteristic of the times.

（3）Reflect characteristic of traffic building.

Reflect spatial characteristic of traffic function.

Reflect architectural style of simplicity.

图 5-14　新广州站“风”——绿叶花街、欢快灵动

Figure 5-14　New Guangzhou Railway Station “Grace” — Green Leaf Flower Street, Cheerful and Lively

图 5-15　北京南站“雅”——天坛概念、饱满恢宏

Figure 5-15　Beijing South Railway Station “Elegance” — Concept form the Temple of Heaven, Luxurious and Magnificent

图 5-16　南京南站“颂”——方正端庄、弘扬文化

Figure 5-16　Nanjing South Railway Station “Glory” —Square and Dignified, Promoting Culture

5. 经济性

必须贯彻强本简末的原则，遵循适合发展阶段的节俭理念，最大限度地降低建设成本：

（1）合理把握客运站规模及标准，不同类型的站房标准有所区别。

（2）充分考虑近、远期结合。

（3）兼顾建设投入与维护成本。

5. Economic Nature

It must carry out the principle of strengthening the fundamental and weakening the trivial, holding a frugal concept suitable for the development stage to minimize construction cost:

（1）Choose reasonable scale and standard for passenger station and set different standards for different types of station buildings.

（2）Take full account of combining short–term and long–term plannings.

（3）Balance construction investment and maintenance cost.

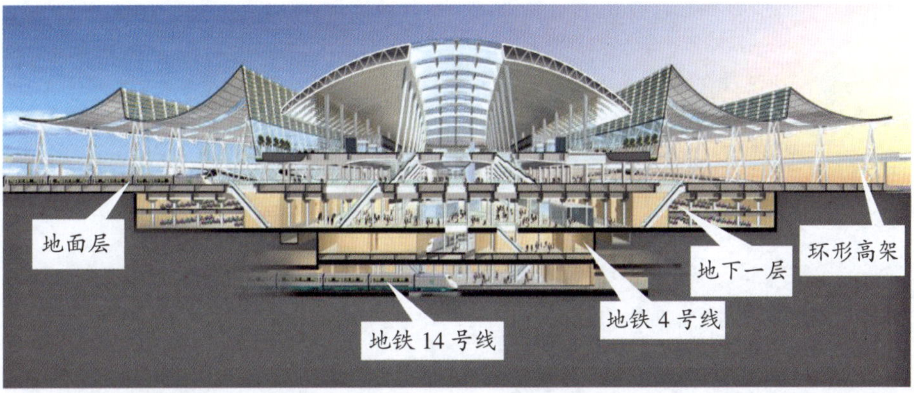

地面层 the ground plane　地铁 14 号线 Metro Line 14　地铁 4 号线 Metro Line 4
地下一层 the underground floor　环形高架 ring interchange

图 5–17　车站规模

Figure 5–17　Station Scale

学习笔记

Study Notes

模块三　课堂练习

Module 3　In-class Exercises

问题 1：根据所学内容说明高速铁路车站的设计特点。

问题 2：总结高速铁路车站设计的主要内容。

问题 3：说明高速铁路车站的建设原则。

Question 1: Explain the design feature of high speed railway station according to what you've learned.

Question 2: Summarize the main content of high speed railway station design.

Question 3: Explain the construction principles of high speed railway station.

课堂练习

In-class Exercises

模块四　课后拓展

收集一个高速铁路车站的资料，或者调研附近的高速铁路车站以说明其设计上的特点。

Module 4　After-class Activity

Collect data of a high speed railway station or research on the nearby high speed railway station to illustrate its design feature.

课后拓展

After-class Activity

任务三　高速铁路车站作业及基本图形

Task 3　Station Operation and Basic Pattern of High Speed Railway

模块一　学前准备

收集资料，了解一下高速铁路车站都有哪几种基本图型。

Module 1　Preparation before Class

Collect data and find out the basic pattern of high speed railway station.

课前学习笔记

Study Notes before Class

模块二　课堂学习

Module 2　In-class Learning

知识点一：高速铁路车站的作业

Key Point 1：High Speed Railway Station Operation

1. 越行站

越行站的作业内容：

（1）办理正线各种列车的通过。

（2）办理速度较快的列车越行，速度较慢的列车不办理旅客乘降作业，只需设两条待避到发线。

（3）不办理客运业务，原则上不设站台。

越行站图型：

1. Overtaking Station

Main operation at overtaking station：

（1） Handling various trains passing through main line.

（2） Generally，it handles faster trains overtaking slower trains，but no passengers on and off operation. Thus，to set two receiving-departure tracks for waiting and avoiding.

（3）Do not handle passenger business，so there is no platform.

Overtaking Station Pattern：

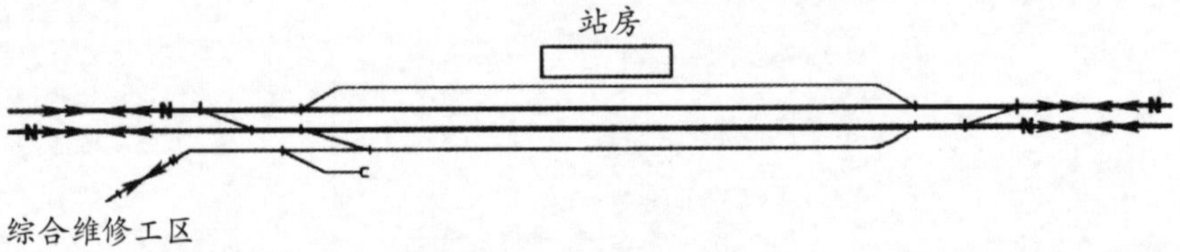

站房 station building　综合维修工区 maintenance area

图 5-18　越行站

Figure 5-18　Overtaking Station

2. 中间站

（1）中间站的作业内容。

① 办理正线各种列车的通过。

②办理停站列车和越行列车进出到发线及旅客上下车。

③办理立即折返列车的终到、始发作业。

④办理始发、终到列车的客运整备（包括清洁、供应物品等）作业和旅客上下车。

2. Intermediate Station

（1）Main operations at intermediate station.

① Deal with various trains passing through main line.

② Arrange stopping trains and overtaking trains in and out of receiving-departure track，and deal with passengers on and off .

③ Handle the final arrival and departure operations of the intermediate turn-back train.

④ Managing the passenger servicing work（including cleaning and supplies，

⑤有综合维修管理区岔线接轨的中间站，在正常情况下，于“天窗”时间内办理检测、维修等列车进出正线作业。

⑥与既有铁路（既有站）有联络线连接的中间站，办理来（去）自既有铁路进入（发出）高速中间站列车（包括高、中速列车，城际动车组）的接发作业。

⑦旅客列车上水作业一般应在始发、终到站进行，在个别情况中，立即折返列车上水作业也有可能在中间站进行。

⑧有其他高速铁路衔接的高速接轨站，除办理以上各项作业外尚有可能办理旅客换乘业务。

（2）中间站的图型。

①对应式图型：中间站台设在到发线外侧或在到发线之间，站台不靠正线。

etc.）in trains which will start from originating station or terminate at destination as well as passengers on and off.

⑤ For intermediate station with comprehensively maintaining base and siding junction, normally train inspection and maintenance are handled at skylight time.

⑥ For an intermediate station interconnecting to the existing railway (station), controlling the arrival–departure operation of trains (including high and medium speed trains, inter–city motor trains units) from (to) existing railway to (from) high speed intermediate station.

⑦ Water feeding operation for passenger trains shall be generally carried out at starting and terminal stations, in some cases, it is also possible for quick turnaround trains to carry out water feeding at intermediate station.

⑧ For the high speed joint station connecting to other high speed railways, managing passenger transferring besides various operations mentioned above.

（2）Basic pattern for intermediate station.

① Corresponding pattern: the middle platform is set outside or between receiving–departure lines, the platform is not close to main line.

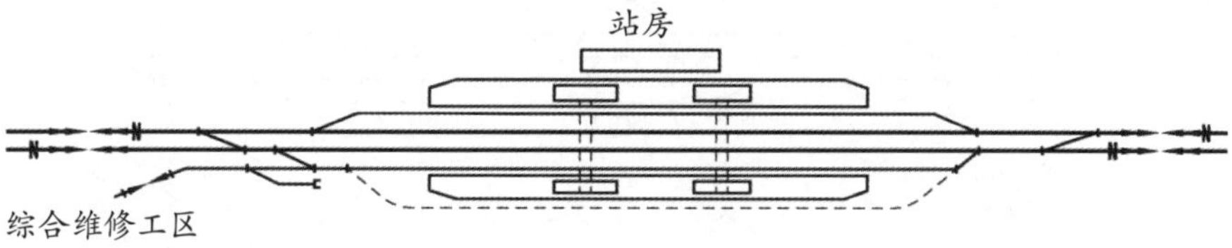

站房 station building　综合维修工区 comprehensive maintenance area

图 5–19　对应式中间高速站

Figure 5–19　Corresponding Pattern Intermediate Station

②岛式图型：中间站台设在正线和到发线之间，站台一侧靠正线，另一侧靠到发线。

有折返作业的中间站：

② Island pattern: the middle platform is set between main line and receiving-departure track, one side of the platform is close to main line and the other side is close to receiving-departure track.

Intermediate station with turnaround operation:

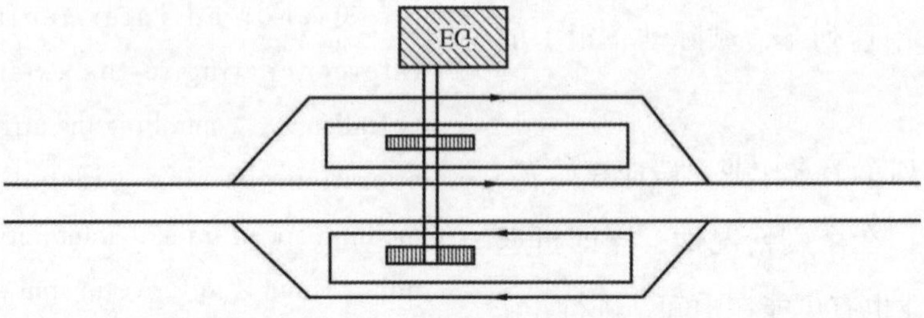

图 5-20　岛式中间高速站

Figure 5-20　Island Pattern Intermediate Station

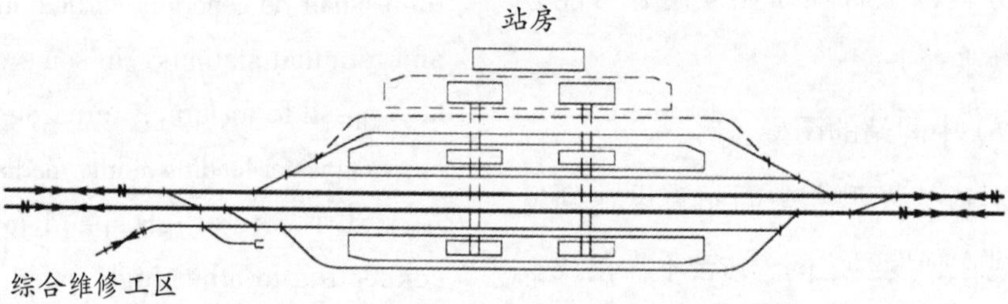

站房 station building　综合维修工区 comprehensive maintenance area

图 5-21　折返作业中间站

Figure 5-21　Intermediate Station with Turnaround Operation

有始发折返作业的中间站：

Intermediate station with arrival-departure turnaround operation:

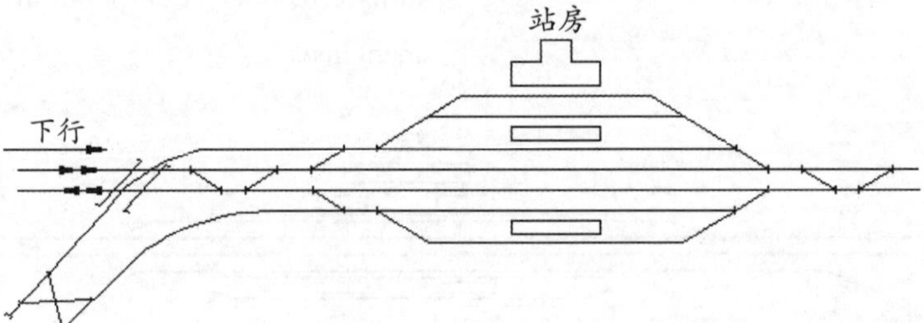

站房 station building　下行 down direction

图 5-22　始发折返作业中间站

Figure 5-22　Intermediate Station with Arrival-Departure Turnaround Operation

3. 枢纽站

枢纽站除了办理上述全部中间站作业外，尚有以下作业：

（1）有较多的始发终到高速列车作业。高速车底（统称动车组）通过走行线进入动车运用维修所（或运用所）进行检修（或小修）存放。动车组从动车运用维修所进入到发线。

（2）有可能进行中速列车列检、上水、更换本务机车（按机车交路）等作业。

（3）枢纽站一般均设有与既有铁路车站之间的高、中速联络线。

联络线的设置一般有两种方式：

① 在枢纽高速站外高速正线出岔后与既有线或既有站连接。其换挂机车和旅客上下车作业，均在既有站办理。

② 在枢纽高速站，出岔平行高速正线引出至既有线或既有站。其换挂机车和旅客上下车作业，可在高速站或既有站办理。一般以在既有站办理为宜，也有少数情况必须在高速站办理。

4. 始发终到站

始发终到站的作业内容：

始发终到站只是相对于一条高速线而言的。跨越该线的列车，在始发终到站仍为通过列车，仅仅是通过的方式可能不同。

始发终到站的作业基本上包括了中

3. Junction Station

In addition to dealing with all intermediate station operations above, junction stations do other operation as follows:

（1） It has more arrival-departure operations for high speed train. The high speed underbody （also called Electric Multiple Unit） goes through running lines into the EMU application maintenance workshop （or EMU workshop） for inspection （or minor repair） storage. EMU enters receiving-departure track from EMU workshop.

（2）It may be possible to do train inspection, water feeding and locomotive changing （according to locomotive routing） for medium speed train.

（3）Generally, junction stations are equipped with high and medium speed connecting lines with existing railway station.

Two ways to set up connecting line:

① Connecting with existing line or station after the high speed main line getting out of turnout at junction station. Locomotive changing and passengers on and off operation are handled at existing station.

② After getting out of the turnout at junction station, the parallel high speed main line can be led out to existing line or station. Locomotive changing and passengers on and off operation can be handled at high speed station or existing station. Generally, it should be handled at existing station, but it must be handled at high speed station in a few cases.

4. Departure Station

Main operation in high speed departure:

High speed departure station is relative

间站、枢纽站的全部作业。有所不同的是，绝大多数列车为始发（或终到）列车，而中间站和枢纽站多数为通过列车。

始发终到站的图型：

to a high speed line. Trains running across the line will still be passing trains at the departure station, and only the way of passing may be different.

Departure station basically carries out all operations of intermediate station and junction station. The majority of trains are originating (or arriving) trains at departure station, while passing trains are mostly of trains at intermediate station and junction station.

Departure Station Pattern:

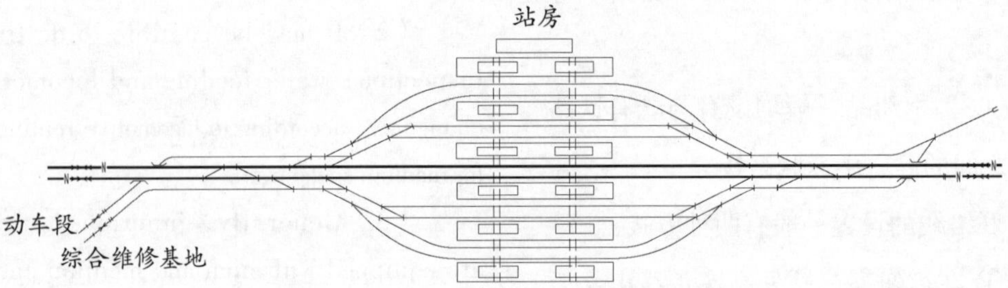

站房 station building　动车段 EMU depot　综合维修基地 comprehensive maintenance base

图 5-23　通过式始发站

Figure 5-23　Through-Type Departure Station

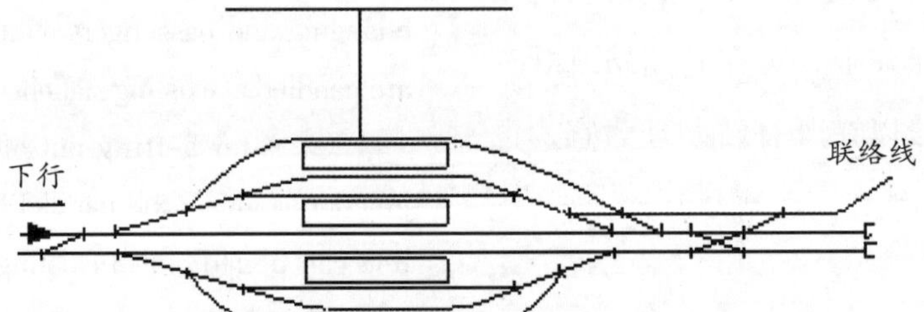

下行 down direction　联络线 connecting line

图 5-24　尽端式始发站

Figure 5-24　Dead-End Departure Station

知识点二：高速铁路车站基本图型适应性分析

图型的选用应当从运营需要出发，考虑行车量、行车组织、客运组织以及安全等方面因素。

（1）中间站基本图型的选用分析。

繁忙高速铁路的中间站应采用对应式图型；只有在运输量少、线路能力富余的线路利用正线作为到发线，停站列车可以不侧向通过道岔时，能采用岛式图型。

（2）折返列车中间站的图型分析。

宜选用对应式图型，因其影响能力大，地形条件可能时也可采用正线外包式图型。

（3）无配线乘降所到发客运量少，影响正线能力，不宜采用。

（4）关于中间站安全线的设置问题。

目前我国高速铁路停站列车进站速度不超过 80 千米 / 时。由于列车自动控制系统完善可靠，除需有隔开进路等特殊情况，可以不设安全线。

（5）终点站图型的选用。

终点站如是利用既有站加改扩建的，不存在选用图型问题。

新建终点站，图型的选择一般应考虑：

①高速铁路网的规划，将来是否另

Key Point 2: Adaptability Analysis of Basic Pattern for High Speed Railway Station

The selection of patterns shall be based on operational needs, considering factors as traffic volume, traffic organization, passenger transport organization, and safety, etc.

(1) Selection analysis of basic pattern for intermediate station.

Busy intermediate station shall adopt corresponding pattern. When lines with less traffic volume and extra railway capacity use main line as the receiving-departure line and stopping trains can go without passing turnout laterally, then island pattern can be adopted.

(2) Pattern analysis for intermediate station with turnaround train.

Select the corresponding pattern. If the influence is great, the straddle-type main track pattern can also be adopted when terrain conditions permit.

(3) Passenger stop point without wiring has low passenger volume, which will affect main line capacity. So, it should not be adopted.

(4) Settings of safety siding for intermediate station.

In China, the stopping train speed of entering high speed railway station is no more than 80 km/h at present. Train automatic control system is complete and reliable. Therefore, except the need for separate access and other special circumstances, there is no need to set safety siding.

(5) Pattern selection for departure station.

If the departure station is a slight

有高速线路引入的可能。

②城市站前广场和城市交通的规划情况。

③动车段与车站的相互位置等因素。

一般情况，通过式图型应是首选方案。如果选用终端式图型，站房和站台以通过式图型布置为宜。

renovation to the existing station，it does not need to select a pattern.

Considerations of the pattern selection for departure station to be newly constructed include：

① The high speed railway network planning and the possibility of introducing other high speed lines in the future.

② The urban station square and urban traffic situation planning.

③ The relative positions of EMU depot and station and other factors.

Generally，through type pattern shall be the first choice. If dead-end pattern is adopted，station building and platform should be arranged in the form of through type pattern.

学习笔记

Study Notes

模块三　课堂练习

问题 1：分别说明高速铁路越行站、中间站、始发终到站、枢纽站各自办理的作业有哪些。

问题 2：说明高速铁路越行站、中间站、始发终到站、枢纽站的基本图型都有哪些。

问题 3：简要进行几种高速铁路车站基本图型的选用分析。

Module 3　In-class Exercises

Question 1: Explain the operations of overtaking station, intermediate station, departure station and junction station, respectively.

Question 2: Illustrate the basic patterns of overtaking station, intermediate station, departure station and junction station, respectively.

Question 3: Briefly explain the selection analysis of several basic patterns for high speed railway station.

课堂练习
In-class Exercises

模块四　课后拓展

根据所学内容，结合高速铁路车站图型分析其特点。

Module 4　After-class Activity

According to what you've learned, try to make analyses of the characteristics of high speed railway station by combining its station pattern.

课后拓展

After-class Activity

任务四　高速铁路车站平、立面的总体布局

Task 4　General Plane and Elevation Layout of High Speed Railway Station

模块一　学前准备

赏析中国高速铁路车站，试着总结高速铁路车站布局、设计特点。

Module 1　Preparation before Class

Appreciate China's high speed railway stations and try to summarize the layout and design features of high speed railway stations.

图 5-25　南京南站

Figure 5-25　Nanjing South Railway Station

图 5-26　北京南站

Figure 5-26　Beijing South Railway Station

图 5-27　三亚站

Figure 5-27　Sanya Railway Station

图 5-28　长沙南站

Figure 5-28　Changsha South Railway Station

图 5-29　哈尔滨西站

Figure 5-29　Harbin West Railway Station

课前学习笔记

Study Notes before Class

知识点一：新建高速铁路车站

Key Point 1: Newly Built High Speed Railway Station

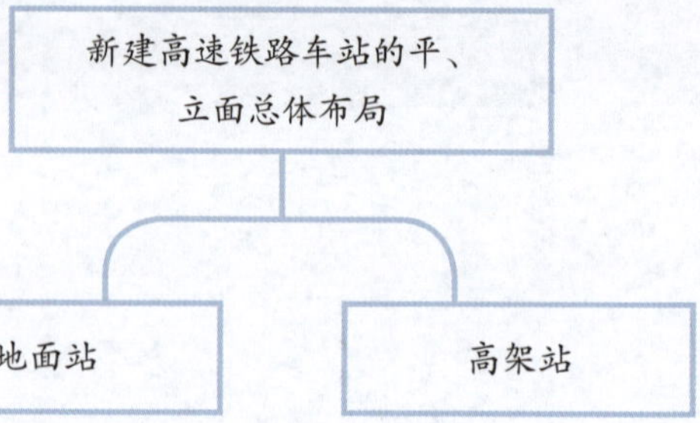

新建高速铁路车站的平、立面总体布局 general plane and elevation layout of newly built high speed railway station　地面站 ground station　高架站 elevated station

图 5-30　全路 TDCS 系统三层网络结构图

Figure 5-30　Three-Layer Network Structure Figure of All-Routes TDCS System

1. 地面站

地面站指建设在一定填土之上的车站。

（1）常规的平、立面总布局方案。

1. Ground Station

Ground station refers to the station built on a certain amount of filling soils.

(1) Ordinary plane and elevation layout scheme.

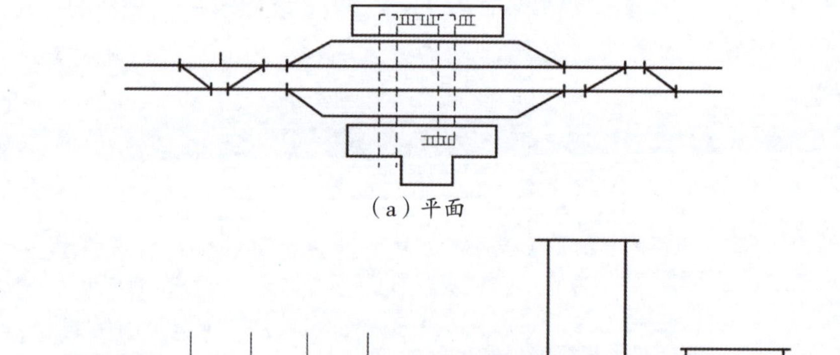

平面 plane　立面 elevation plane

图 5-31　常规地面车站布局

Figure 5-31　Ordinary Layout of Ground Station

（2）候车室为高架于车站之上的平、立面总布置方案。

（2）General plane and elevation layout of the waiting room elevated above station.

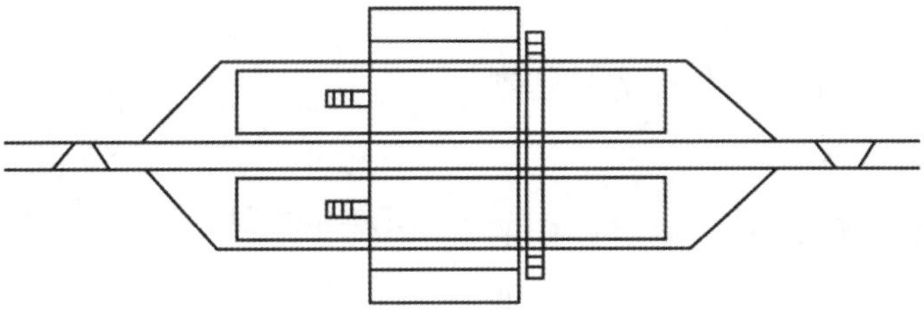
（a）平面

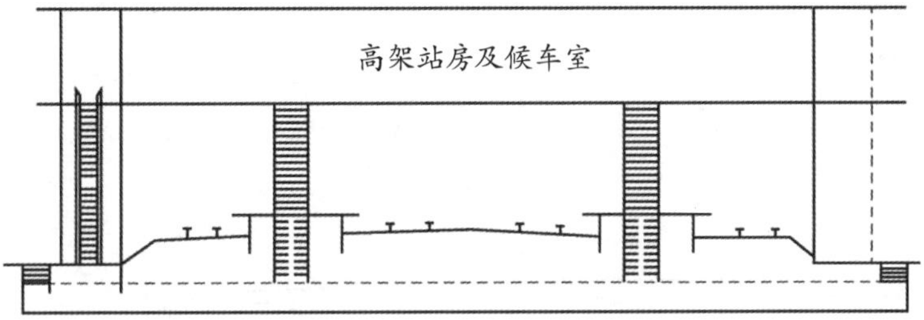

（b）立面

平面 plane　立面 elevation　高架站房及候车室 elevated station building and waiting room

图 5-32　候车室高架于车站之上的车站布局

Figure 5-32　Station Layout with Waiting Room Elevated Above Station

2. 高架站

因新建车站两端线路与多处道路交叉而设计为高架线路，该车站被称为高架站。

2. Elevated Station

Lines at both ends of the newly-built station are designed as elevated lines due to crossing with many tracks. This kind of station is called an elevated station.

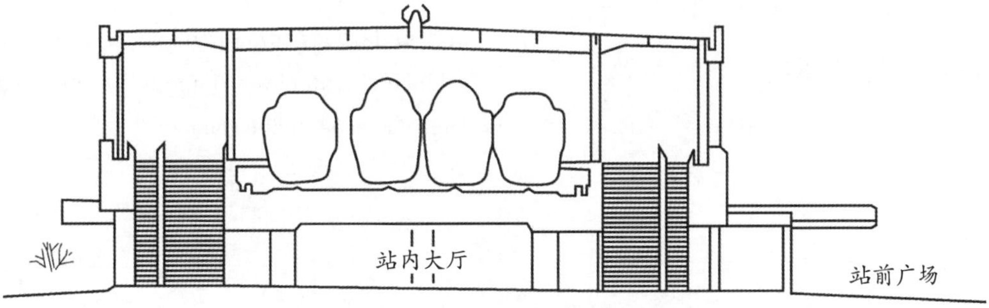

站内大厅 station hall　站前广场 station square

图 5-33　TDCD 高架站布局（立面）

Figure 5-33　Layout of TDCD Elevated Station （Elevation）

知识点二：与既有站紧靠并列设置的高速站

Key Point 2：High Speed Station Adjacent to Existing Station

1. 高速站为地面站，与既有站基本等高的立面布局方案

1. High Speed Station is a Ground Station，which is Basically the Same Equal-Height Elevation Layout as the Existing Station

（1）立面布局采用与地道连接的“低进低出”方案。对高速站而言，此方案与新建高速站的形式相同，只是旅客要横越既有站。

（1）Elevation layout adopts the “low in and low out” scheme connected with underpass tunnel. For high speed station, this scheme is the same as newly built high speed station，but passengers have to cross the existing station.

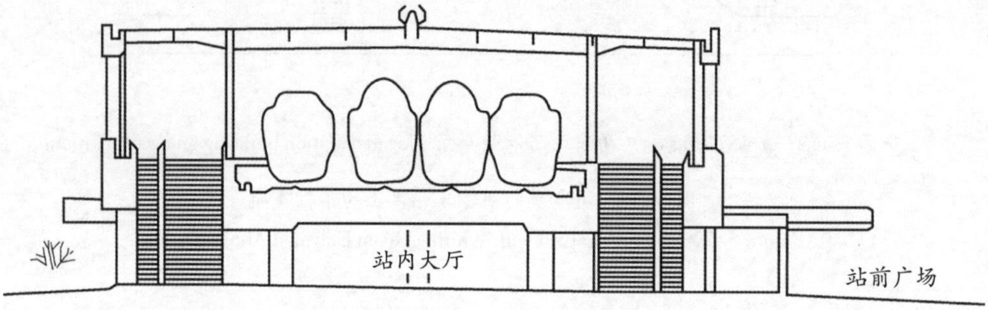

图 5-34 “低进低出”方案布局

Figure 5-34 Layout of “Low In and Low Out” Scheme

（2）立面布局采用以高架通廊（或高架候车室）进站、以地道出站的“高进低出”方案。这种方案适用于客运量大的大型枢纽客运站。

（2）Elevation layout adopts the “high in and low out” scheme with elevated corridor （or elevated waiting room） to enter station and underpass tunnel to exit station. This scheme is suitable for large hub station with large passenger traffic volume.

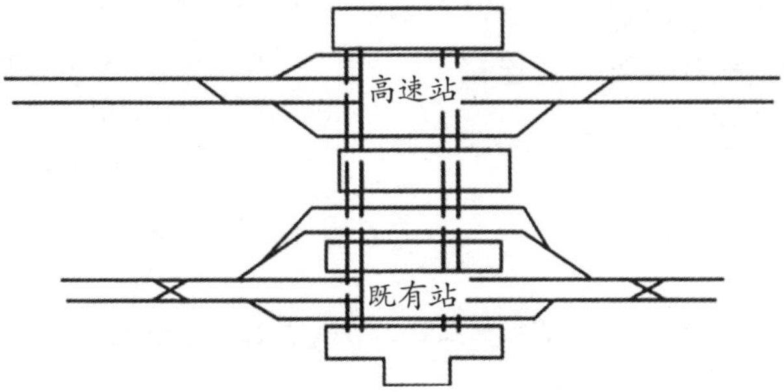

高速站 high speed railway station　既有站 exsiting station

图 5-35　南京高速站与既有站地铁 1 号线示意图

Figure 5-35　Figure of Nanjing High Speed Station and Existing Station Metro Line 1

2. 高架站与既有站紧靠并列的高速站布局方案

将高架站桥下净空作为高速车站旅客候车室或站厅。与既有站以地道连接，高速客车与普速客车共用进出站地道，如图 5-36 所示。

2. Arrangement Scheme for High Speed Station with the Elevated Station Adjacent to Existing Station

Use clearance under the elevated station bridge as waiting room or station hall for high speed passengers. It is connected with the existing station by underpass tunnel. High speed trains and normal speed trains share entering and exiting underpass tunnel, as shown in Figure 5-36.

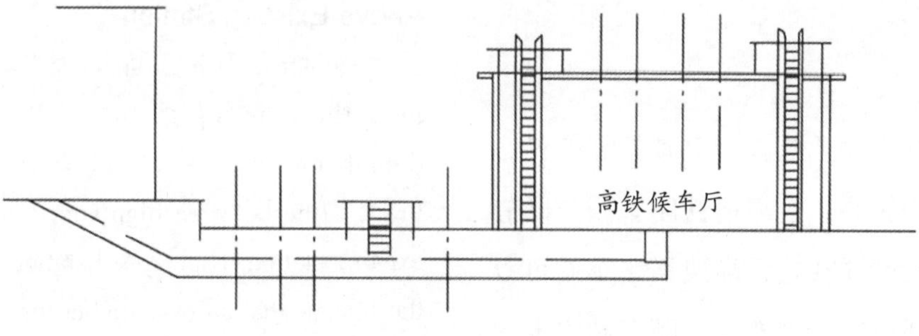

高铁候车厅 high speed rail waiting room

图 5-36　高架站与既有站紧靠并列的布置方案一

Figure 5-36　Arrangement Scheme 1 of Elevated Station Adjacent to Existing Station

乘坐高速铁路列车的旅客利用既有站房候车，立面布局采用高架走廊连接高速站“高进高出”的方案。如图 5-37 所示。

High speed passengers use the existing station building as waiting room. The elevation layout adopts the scheme of "high in and high out" which uses elevated corridor to connect high speed station. As shown in Figure 5-37.

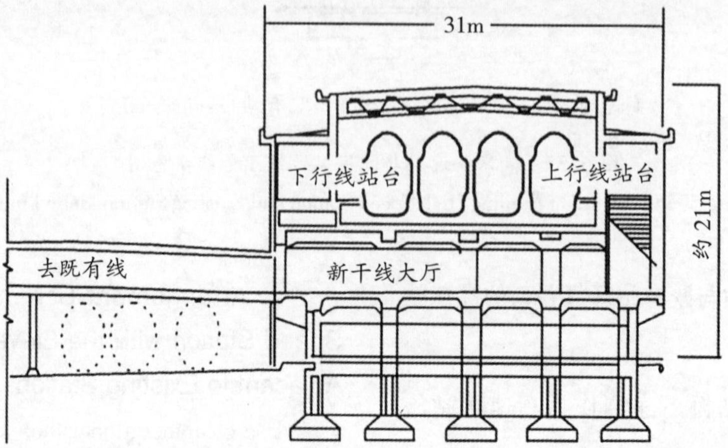

下行线站台 down track platform　上行线站台 up track platform　去既有线 departing existing line
新干线大厅 Shinkansen hall

图 5-37　高架站与既有站紧靠并列的布置方案二

Figure 5-37　Arrangement Scheme 2 of Elevated Station Adjacent to Existing Station

知识点三：高架建于既有站之上的车站

Key Point 3: Elevated Station Built Above Existing Station

在既有站附近修建高速铁路车站，拆迁费用较高，且高速铁路车站与既有站之间有岔线相连，高速铁路车站可以采用全部或部分高架建于既有站之上的方案。如图 5-38 所示，其中 1~5 为中、普速车场站台，6~8 为高速车场站台。

Construct a high speed railway station near the existing station will cost huge demolition expense, and there will be a branch line between high speed station and existing station. High speed station can adopt the scheme that all or partial of the high speed station is built above the existing station. As shown in Figure 5-38, among which 1~5 are platforms of medium and normal speed yard, 6~8 are platforms of high speed yard.

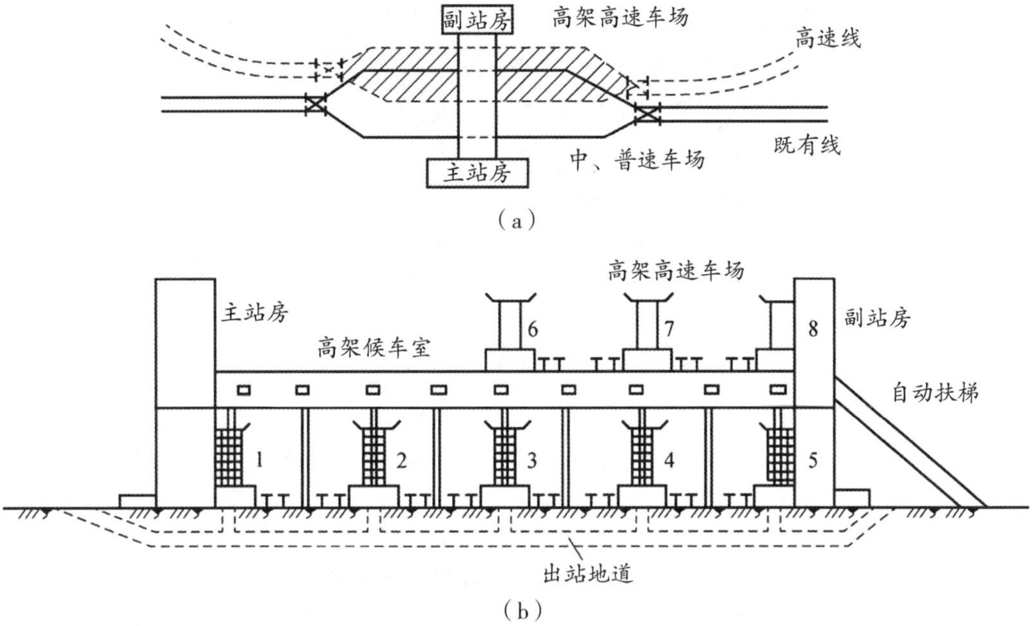

副站房 auxiliary station building 主站房 main station building 高架高速车场 elevated high speed yard
中、普速车场 medium and normal speed yard 既有线 existing railway 高速线 high speed railway
高架候车室 elevated waiting room 自动扶梯 escalator 出站地道 exiting underpass tunnel

图 5–38 既有站上方设高架高速列车车站平、立面布置局

Figure 5–38 Plane and Elevation Layouts of Elevated High Speed Train Station above Existing Station

知识点四：利用既有站的车站

1. 高、普速共车场的车站

全部利用既有站、高速正线在站外与既有正线连接；利用既有正线进站，高速正线不直接引入既有站的车站，称为高、普速共车场的车站。

Key Point 4：Make Use of Existing Station

1. Station of High and Normal Speed Shared Yard

Use all existing station and high speed main line to connect with existing main line outside the station; use existing main line to enter station and high speed main line is not directly led to the existing station. All the stations above can be called stations of high and normal speed shared yard.

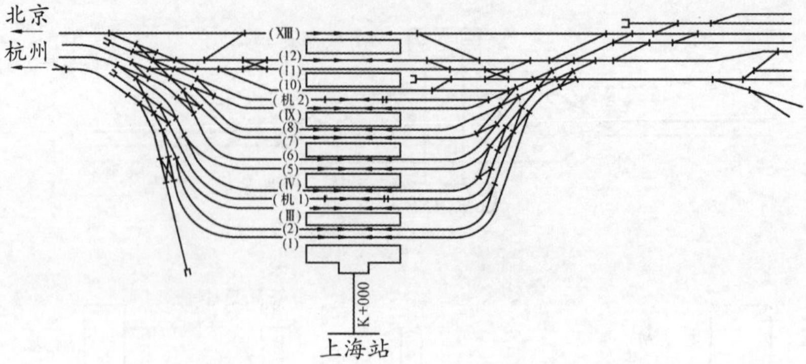

北京 Beijing　杭州 Hangzhou　上海站 Shanghai station

图 5-39　上海站布局

Figure 5-39　Layout of Shanghai Railway Station

2. 高、普速分车场的车站

利用既有站改扩建，将高速正线直接引入车站，与既有正线有平行进路通过咽喉的车站，称为高、普速分车场的车站。如北京站（图 5-40）、东京站（图 5-41）。

2. Station of High and Normal Speed Branch Yard

Station of high and normal speed branch yard makes use of reconstruction and renovation of the existing station, introduces high speed main line directly into station, and has a parallel route to the existing main line going through throat. For example, Beijing Railway Station (Figure 5-40) and Tokyo Railway Station (Figure 5-41).

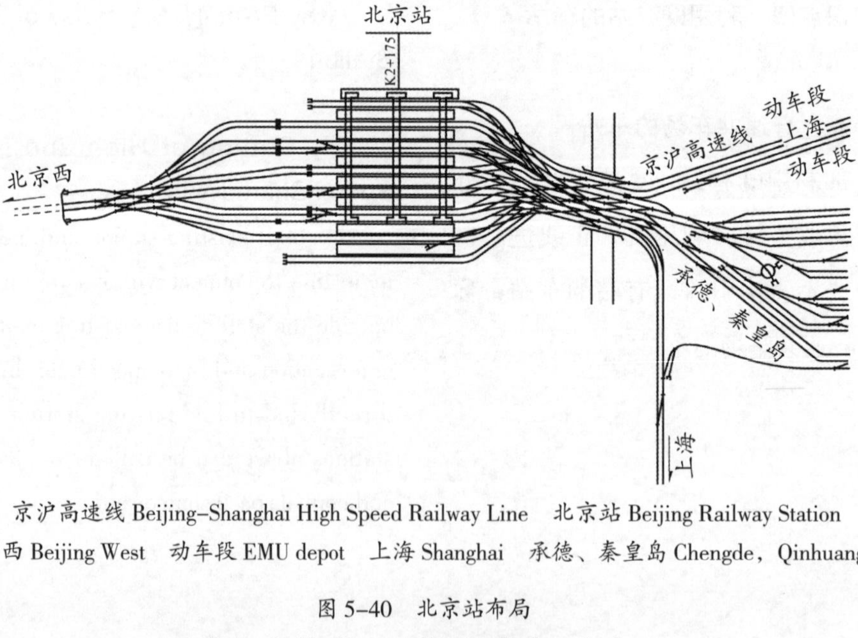

京沪高速线 Beijing-Shanghai High Speed Railway Line　北京站 Beijing Railway Station

北京西 Beijing West　动车段 EMU depot　上海 Shanghai　承德、秦皇岛 Chengde, Qinhuangdao

图 5-40　北京站布局

Figure 5-40　Layout of Beijing Railway Station

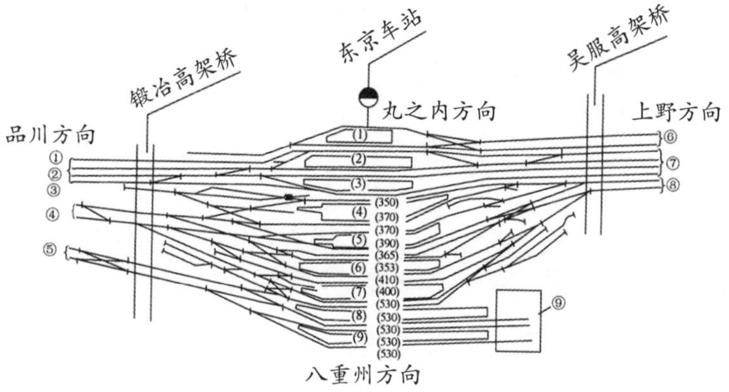

品川方向 to Shinagawa　锻冶高架桥 Kajiya Viaduct　东京车站 Tokyo Railway Station
丸之内方向 to Marunouchi　吴服高架桥 Gofuko Viaduct　上野方向 to Ueno　八重州方向 to Yaesu

图 5–41　东京站布局

Figure 5–41　Layout of Tokyo Railway Station

3. 地下站

受拥挤市区所限，不能在地面建站，因此选择建地下站。与高架站一样，它是利用立体空间建设的高速车站。如东京市上野地下站（图 5–42）。

3. Underground Station

Due to the limitation of crowded urban areas, it is impossible to build stations on the ground, so underground stations are chosen. They are built by using three-dimensional space as the elevated station, e.g. the Ueno Underground Station in Tokyo (Figure 5–42).

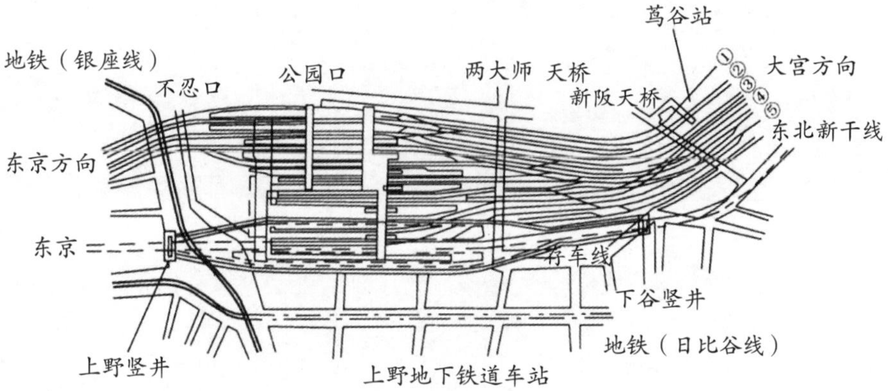

地铁（银座线）Metro（Ginza Line）　地铁（日比谷线）Metro（Hibiya Line）　东京方向 to Tokyo
东京 Tokyo　上野竖井 Ueno Shaft　不忍口 Shinobazuguchi　公园口 park entrance　两大师 Ryoudaishi
天桥 over-bridge　新阪天桥 Shinzaka Over-bridge　莺谷站 Uguisudani Station　大宫方向 to Oomiya
东北新干线 Tohoko Shinkansen　下谷竖井 Shitaya Shaft　存车线 storage siding
上野地下铁道车站 Ueno Subway Station

图 5–42　东京市上野地下站布局

Figure 5–42　Layout of Ueno Underground Station in Tokyo

学习笔记

Study Notes

模块三　课堂练习

问题 1：针对高速铁路车站的布局特点，做小组讨论。

问题 2：客运专线车站为地面站，与既有站基本等高且并列布置。简述“低进低出”方案。

问题 3：客运专线车站为地面站，与既有站基本等高且并列布置。简述“高进低出”方案。

Module 3　In-class Exercises

Question 1：Make group discussion on the layout characteristics of high speed railway station.

Question 2：The passenger dedicated line station is on the ground and basically equal in height and parallel to the existing station. Briefly describe the scheme of “low in and low out”.

Question 3：The passenger dedicated line station is on the ground and basically equal in height and parallel to the existing station. Briefly describe the scheme of “high in and low out”.

课堂练习
In-class Exercises

模块四 课后拓展

分析当地某一高速铁路车站平、立面的布局特点。

Module 4 After-class Activity

Analyze the plane and elevation layout characteristics of a local high speed railway station.

课后拓展

After-class Activity

项目六　高速铁路客运设备及段、所布置

Project 6　Passenger Transport Equipment and Setting of Depot and Workshop for High Speed Railway

任务一　客运设施

Task 1　Passenger Transport Equipment

模块一　学前准备

搜集离你最近的高铁站名称，进入车站熟悉车站布局并拍以下照片：车站整体外观、候车厅、站台、跨线通道（如果站内有天桥、地道）等。

Module 1　Preparation before Class

Collect the name of high speed railway station nearest to you，enter the station and get familiar with its layout. Take following photos：overall appearance of station，waiting hall，platform，cross–line access road （if there are over–bridge and underpass tunnel in station），etc.

课前学习笔记
Study Notes before Class

模块二 课堂学习

知识点一：旅客站房地面高程与站台面高程的关系

如图 6–1 所示，旅客站房地面高程与站台面高程的关系有下列三种形式：

线平式：站房地面高程与站台面高程相差很小或相同。

线上式：站房地面高程高于站台面高程。

线下式：站房地面高程低于站台面高程。

Module 2 In–class Learning

Key Point 1：Relationship between Passenger Station Building Elevation and Platform Elevation

As shown in Figure 6–1，there are three forms of relationship between passenger station building elevation and platform elevation：

Track level：the difference between station building elevation and platform elevation is very small or the same.

Above track level：station building elevation is higher than platform elevation.

Below track level：station building elevation is lower than platform elevation.

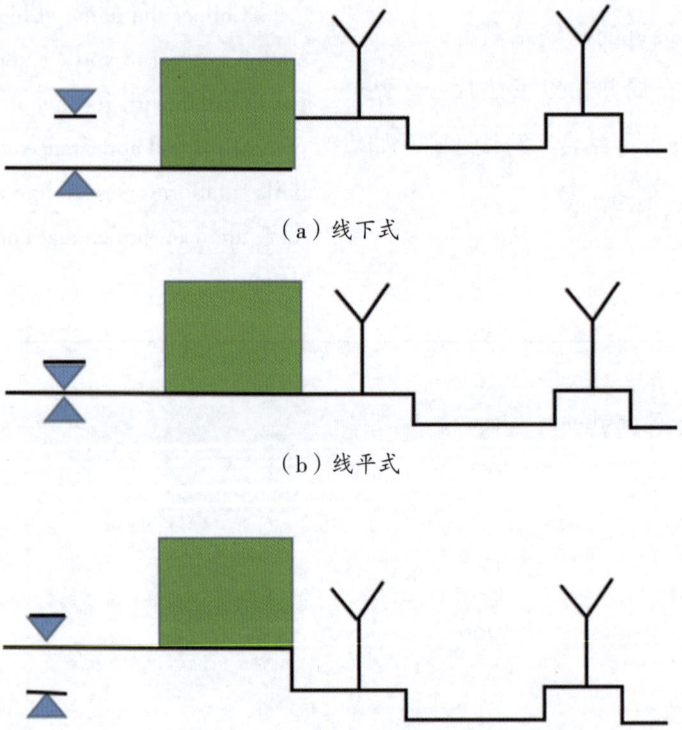

（a）线下式

（b）线平式

（c）线上式

线下式 below track level　线平式 track level　线上式 above track level

图 6–1　旅客站房地面高程与站台面高程的关系

Figure 6–1　Relationship between Passenger Station Building Elevation and Platform Elevation

知识点二：旅客站台

Key Point 2：Passenger Platform

1. 站台上旅客（及工作人员）的安全距离

1. Safety Distance for Passengers (and Staff) on Platform

当站台一侧为正线，并有不停站的高速列车通过时，因环绕车体的气流压力对人体安全有影响，需要加宽安全距离。图 6–2 为日本东海道新干线热海站测试的结果。热海站是不设到发线的车站，站台设在正线两侧外，单面使用。

When one side of the platform is a main line and there are non-stop high speed trains passing, the safe distance should be widened due to the influence of air pressure around vehicle body on human body safety. Figure 6–2 shows the test results of Atami Station of Tokaido Shinkansen in Japan. Atami Station has no receiving-departure track and the platform is set up outside both sides of main line, and one side is used.

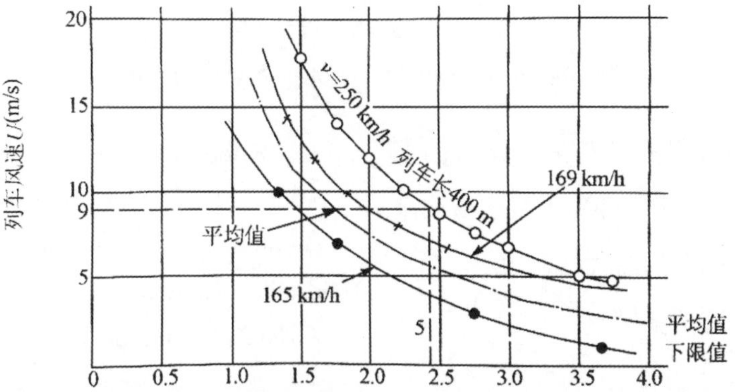

列车风速 train wind speed　平均值 average value　列车长 train length　下限值 low limit

图 6–2　距离车体侧面的距离

Figure 6–2　Distance from Side of Vehicle Body

为安全起见，热海、神户等站在距站台边缘 2.5 米处安装了带有自动门的防护栅栏，如图 6–3 所示。

For safety, stations in Atami, Kobe and other places have installed safety railings with automatic doors 2.5m from platform edge, as shown in Figure 6–3.

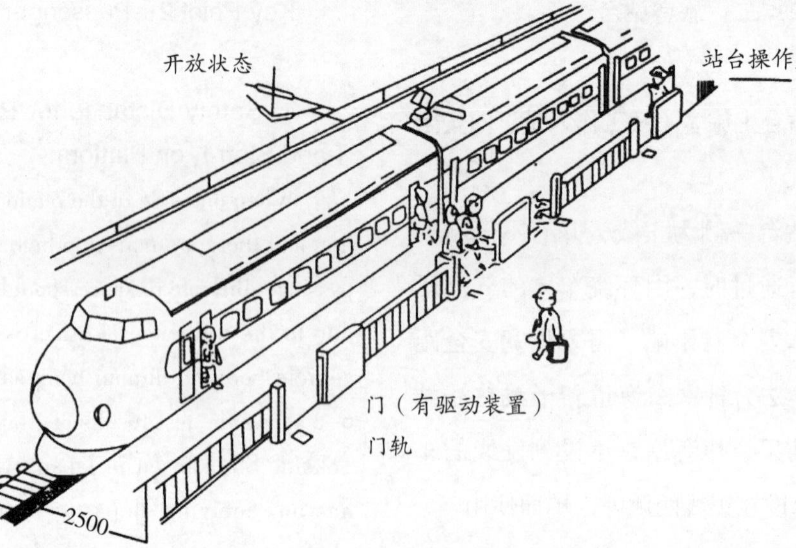

开放状态 in open status 门（有驱动装置）door（with driving device）
门轨 door rail 站台操作盘 platform operating console

图 6-3 新干线热海站自动安全门

Figure 6-3 Automatic Safety Door of Atami Station on Shinkansen Line

当装设安全防护栅栏后，站台的安全距离可以为 2.0 米。如新干线的横滨车站，在有通过列车的岛式站台边缘 2.0 米处设了同样的防护栅栏。

Safety distance of the platform can be 2.0m with safety railings. For example, Yokohama Station on Shinkansen line has installed safety railings, 2.0 m from the edge of island platform with passing trains.

2. 旅客站台长度的确定

如图 6-4 所示，旅客站台长度是按列车长度加前后富余长度确定的。一般按动车组 16 辆编组计，每辆车长度 26.0 米，车底长度 420 米，站台长度应考虑动车组前后各加 15 米的停车余量，确定旅客站台长度为 450 米。只停留 8 辆编组动车组的车站站台长按 230 米设置，困难条件下不应小于 220 米。

2. Determine the Length of Passenger Platform

As shown in Figure 6-4, the length of passenger platform is determined by the train length plus the extra lengths both front and back. Platform length is calculated by 16-cars EMU. With each car 26m long, the bottom length is 420m. Therefore, the platform shall be 450m long, taking into account 15m parking space in front and back of the EMU. Platform shall be 230m for railway station with only 8-cars EMU, and being at least 220m in difficult cases.

图 6–4 旅客站台长度

Figure 6–4 Length of Passenger Platform

3. 旅客站台宽度的确定

根据《高速铁路设计规范（试行）》，旅客站台宽度应根据车站性质、站台类型、客流密度、安全退避距离、站台出入口宽度等因素确定，见表 6–1。

3. Determine the Width of Passenger Platform

According to "The Code for Design of High speed Railway （for Trial Implementation）", the width of passenger platform shall be determined by factors as station nature, platform type, density of passenger flow, safety draw-back distance, width of platform entrance and exit, etc., as shown in Chart 6–1.

表 6–1 旅客站台宽度

Chart 6–1 Width of Passenger Platform

名称	特大及大型站（米）	中型站（米）	小型站（米）
站房（行车室）突出部分边缘至站台边缘距离	15.0~20.0	12.0~15.0	≥ 8.0 通过对站面站房处 ≥ 10.0
岛式中间站台	11.5~12.0	10.5~12.0	10.0~11.0
侧式中间站台	8.5~9.0	7.5~8.0	7.0~8.0

名称 name 特大及大型站（米）super-large or large station（m） 中型站（米）medium station （m） 小型站（米）small station（m） 站房（行车室）突出部分边缘至站台边缘距离 distance between the margins of projecting part of station building（edge room）and platform edge 通过对站面站房处 through the opposite station building 岛式中间站台 island intermediate platform 侧式中间站台 side intermediate platform

注：当通道出入口设于基本站台站房范围以外地段时，基本站台宽度不小于侧式中间站台标准。

Note：When the access road entrance and exit are set up outside the station building，the width of passenger platform shall not be less than the width of side intermediate platform.

4. 旅客站台高度的确定

为便于旅客上下车，站台高度应高出轨面 1.25 米。

站台结构：高度 1.25 米的站台宜采用现浇或预制钢筋混凝土站台墙。当站台下有人员通行时应采用图 6–5 的形式。

4. Determine the Height of Passenger Platform

Platform shall be 1.25m higher than rail plane to facilitate passengers on and off.

Platform structure: platform wall with a platform height of 1.25m should be constructed as cast–in–situ or prefabricated reinforced concrete platform wall. platform wall in Figure 6–5 shall be adopted when there are pedestrians passing under platform.

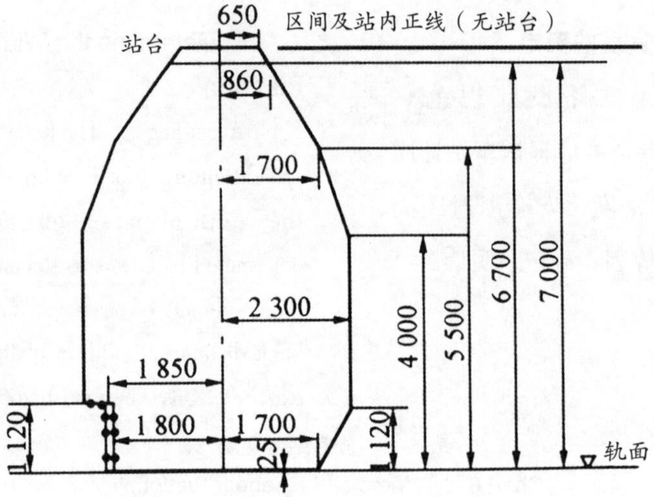

站台 platform　区间及站内正线（无站台）section of a normal route and mainline in the station

轨面 rail plane

图 6–5　站台下有人通行的站台墙和排水沟形式图（单位：毫米）

Figure 6–5　Form Figure of Platform Wall and Drainage Ditch for Platform with Pedestrians Passing（Unit：mm）

知识点三：旅客跨线通道的设置

天桥、地道的宽度应根据客流密度确定。旅客进出站的组织应避免通道内有对流现象。通道的宽度主要取决于一次下车或同时进站的最大旅客人数。大型站进、出站通道应分别设置，当聚集

Key Point 3: Setting of Passenger Cross–Line Access Road

The width of overpass and underpass shall be determined by passenger flow density. The organization of passengers entering and exiting station shall avoid counter flow in access road. The width of access road mainly

人数在 10000~30000 人及以上时，通道的宽度不应小于 8.0 米；当聚集人数在 3000~6000 人时，不应小于 6.0 米。聚集人数在 600 人以下的小型站，通道的宽度也不应小于 4.0 米。如图 6-6 所示。

旅客进出站通道均宜设双侧出、入口通向各站台，以方便旅客出入。因位置或其他原因，站台两个出、入口的客流量并不对等。

depends on the maximum number of passengers getting off at one time or entering station at the same time. Access entrance and exit in large station shall be set up separately. When the number of passengers is 10000 ~ 30000 and above, the width of access shall not be less than 8.0m; when the number of passengers is 3000~6000, the width of access shall not be less than 6.0m. The width of access shall not be less than 4.0m for small station with passengers less than 600, as shown in Figure 6-6.

Passenger station access should be set with bidirectional entrances and exits to each platform for convenience. Due to location or other reasons, the passenger flow between two entrances and exits is not equal.

图 6-6　旅客跨线通道

Figure 6-6　Passenger Cross-Line Access Road

高速铁路车站旅客站台出入口宽度设置见表 6–2。

The width of passenger platform entrance and exit for high speed railway station, see Chart 6–2.

表 6–2　旅客站台出入口宽度

Chart 6–2　Width of Entrance and Exit for Passenger Platform

名称	特大及大型站（m）	中型站（m）	小型站（m）
基本站台、岛式中间站台	5.0~5.5	4.0~5.0	3.5~4.0
侧式中间站台	5.0	4.0	3.5~4.0

名称 name　特大及大型站（m）super–large or large station（m）　中型站（m）medium station（m）
小型站（m）small station（m）　基本站台、岛式中间站台 basic platform，island intermediate platform
侧式中间站台 side intermediate platform

知识点四：高速车站名称规定

Key Point 4：Provisions on Naming High Speed Station

（1）车站名称应与车站所在地地名一致，且在全国范围内不应有相同的车站名称，如图 6–7 所示。

（1）Station name shall be consistent with the place name where the station is located. There shall not be the same station name nationwide, as shown in Figure 6–7.

图 6–7　普者黑站位于中国云南省文山壮族苗族自治州丘北县境内

Figure 6–7　Puzhehei Station is located in Qiubei County，Wenshan Zhuang and Miao Autonomous Prefecture，Yunnan Province，China

（2）车站位于城市城区或近郊的，应使用该城市的名称命名，如图 6–8 所示。当车站位于县、乡（镇）或村所在地时，应当以县、乡（镇）或村庄的名称命名。

（2）If the station is located in urban or suburban area of a city，it shall be named after the city，as shown in Figure 6–8. When the station is located in county，township（town）or village，it shall be named after the county，township（town）or village.

图 6–8　北京南站位于中国北京丰台区

Figure 6–8　Beijing South Railway Station is located in Fengtai District，Beijing，China

（3）当城市城区或近郊设有多个车站时，其中办理客运业务最主要的车站使用该城市的名称命名，其他主要车站可使用该城市名称加该站实际地理位置的方位词（东、南、西、北）命名，也可使用车站当地小名命名。

（4）城市内非主要或位于城市远郊区的车站，不应使用城市名称或城市名称加地理方位词的方式命名。

（3）When a number of stations are set up in urban or suburban areas of a city，the station that handles most of the passenger transportation business shall be named after the city. Other major stations may be named after the city plus actual geographical location word（east，south，west，north），or by the local nickname.

（4）Stations that are not the main one or in outskirts of a city shall not be named by the city name or the city name plus geographical location word.

学习笔记

Study Notes

模块三　课堂练习

讨论表 6-1 旅客站台宽度的数据如何确定。

Module 3　In-class Exercises

Discuss how to determine the data in Chart 6-1 Width of Passenger Platform.

课堂练习

In-class Exercises

模块四　课后拓展

Module 4　After-class Activity

搜集云南省境内高速铁路车站的名称，分析其命名规律。

Collect names of high speed railway stations in Yunnan Province and analyze their naming rules.

课后拓展

After-class Activity

任务二　段、所、区平面布置设计

Task 2　Plane Layout and Design of Depot，Workshop and Section

模块一　学前准备

从网上搜集离你最近的动车段总平面布置图，有条件的可到现场进行拍照。

Module 1　Preparation before Class

Search online and collect the plane layout of EMU depot closest to you. Take photos at the scene if possible.

课前学习笔记
Study Notes before Class

知识点一：动车段（检修基地）、所平面布置

1. 检修修程及范围分类

我国高速动车组实行计划预防修，有运用检修和定期检修两个类别。根据修程、修制的不同，各型 CRH 的检修主要分为一级、二级、三级、四级、五级五个等级，其中一、二级检修属于运用检修，在动车运用所进行，如图 6-9 所示；三、四、五级检修属于定期检修，在动车检修基地或主机厂进行，如图 6-10 所示。

Key Point 1: Plane Layout of EMU Depot (Maintenance Base) and Workshop

1. Classification of Locomotive Repair and Scope

China's high speed EMU adopt planned preventive maintenance, which is divided into operational maintenance and regular maintenance. Classifications of locomotive repair and repair system of different CRH types mainly include five grades, of which Class 1 & 2 maintenance belong to operational maintenance and are carried out in EMU workshop, as shown in Figure 6-9; Class 3, 4 & 5 maintenance belong to regular maintenance and are carried out at EMU base or main engine factory, as shown in Figure 6-10.

图 6-9　郑州东站动车运用所

Figure 6-9　EMU Workshop of Zhengzhou East Railway Station

图 6-10 位于华中地区第一大动车检修基地的武汉动车段

Figure 6-10 Wuhan EMU Depot，Largest EMU Maintenance Base in Central China

2. 动车组检修工艺流程

动车组采用全密封、不摘钩、整列动车段检查、整备和维修，也可根据需要摘钩成两个半列入库进行检修，这是一种全新的维修模式。

根据高速动车组入段作业的性质，大致可分为三种维修流程（注：轮对踏面检查每四天进行一次，不落轮镟轮间隔 10×10^4km~12×10^4km），如图 6-11 所示。

2. Maintenance Process of EMU

EMU adopts fully sealed，coupling，whole EMU depot inspection，servicing and maintenance. It can also be uncoupled into two and a half parts for maintenance according to its needs. This is a brand-new maintenance mode.

According to the nature of high speed EMU accessing depot operation，there are roughly three maintenance processes（note：wheelset tread inspection is carried out every 4 days and the space between under-floor wheel lathe is 10×10^4km~12×10^4km），as shown in Figure 6-11.

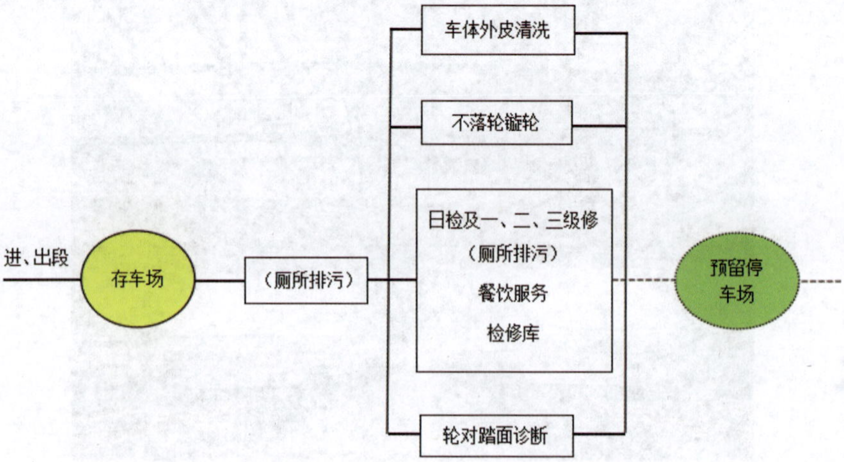

进、出段 access depot　存车场 stabling yard　厕所排污 toilet sewage
车体外皮清洗 vehicle external cleaning　不落轮镟轮 under-floor wheel lathe
日检及一、二、三级修 daily inspection and Class-1，2，3 maintenance　餐饮服务 catering service
检修库 maintenance workshop　轮对踏面诊断 wheelset tread diagnosis　预留停车场 reserved parking lot

图 6-11　动车组检修工艺流程
Figure 6-11　Maintenance Process of EMU

3. 动车段总平面布置方案

总平面布置可归纳为以下三种基本类型方案：

（1）纵列式方案。

纵列式方案，即存车场与检修库成纵向排列布置。该类方案由于基本上可实现流水作业程序而被广泛地采用。国外纵列式布置的动车段有如日本上越新干线的新澜动车段、东海道新干线的东京动车段、山阳新干线的博多动车段、仙台动车段以及德国汉堡动车段等。我国京沪高速铁路设计的上海动车段亦为纵列式，如图 6-12 所示。广州动车基地同样是纵列式。

3. General Layout of EMU Depot

The general layout can be summarized into the following three basic types of scheme：

（1）Longitudinal layout scheme.

Longitudinal layout scheme refers to stabling yard and maintenance workshop are longitudinally arranged. This kind of layout is widely adopted because it can basically realize the flow process. Some longitudinally arranged EMU depots in foreign countries include：Shinlan EMU Depot of Japan's Joetsu Shinkansen，Tokyo EMU Depot of Tokaido Shinkansen，Hakata EMU Depot and Sendai EMU Depot of Sanyo Shinkansen，Germany Hamburg EMU Depot，etc. Shanghai EMU Depot of China's Beijing-Shanghai high speed railway also adopts longitudinal layout，as shown in Figure 6-12，same to Guangzhou EMU Base .

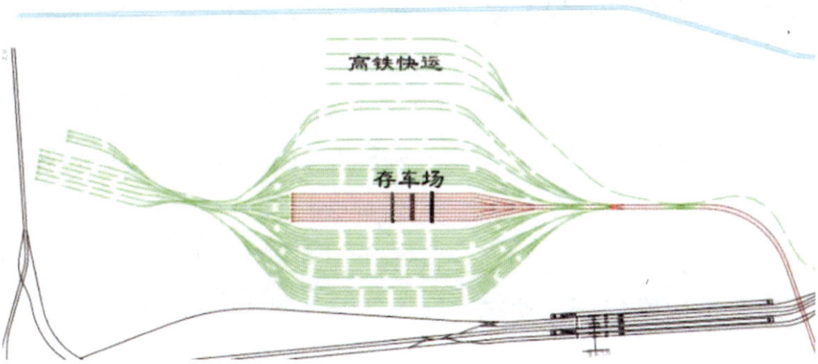

高铁客运 high speed rail passenger　存车场 stabling yard

图 6-12　上海动车段总平面布置采纵列式方案

Figure 6-12　The General Layout of Shanghai EMU Depot Adopts Longitudinal Layout

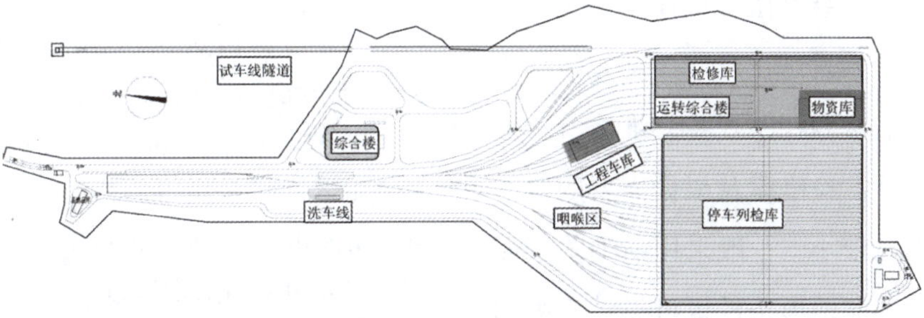

试车线隧道 test line tunnel　综合楼 multiple-use building　洗车线 car wash line
咽喉区 throat area　工程车库 engineering garage　检修库 maintenance workshop
运转综合楼 operation multiple-use building　物资库 material storehouse
停车列检库 parking train inspection garage

图 6-13　成都动车段总平面布置采横列式方案

Figure 6-13　The General Layout of Chengdu EMU Depot Adopts Horizontal Layout

（2）横列式方案。

横列式方案即存车场与检修库成横向并列布置，如成都动车段，见图 6-13 所示。法国巴黎的沙地翁动车段，距大西洋高速铁路始发站蒙帕纳斯约 5 千米。

（3）其他形式方案。

其他形式方案包括存车场与检修库部分横列、部分纵列或其他受场地限制而形成的总平面布置方案。如日本的大阪第二车辆所，经逐步扩建成为特殊的

(2) Horizontal layout scheme.

Horizontal layout refers to the stabling yard and maintenance workshop which are horizontally arranged in parallel, e. g. Chengdu EMU Depot, as shown in Figure 6-13. Chatillon EMU depot in Paris, France is about 5km away from the departure station—Montparnasse, of the TGV-Atlantque high speed railway.

(3) Other forms of layout scheme.

Other forms of layout scheme include partial horizontal, or partial longitudinal layout

布置形式，法国的兰地高速动车段是随地形而布置的。

知识点二：动车运用维修所、动车运用所平面布置

1. 动车运用维修所平面布置

动车运用维修所一般设于始发终到列车较多的始发站，有配属动车组，承担日检、临修和存车任务。维修所一般设有 2 线日常检修库及根据需要的存车线。其规模较小，一般采用横列式平面布置，为适应地形条件也可设计为纵列式布置。

2. 动车运用所平面布置

动车运用所不配属动车组、不做动车组的日检作业，只承担存车任务，必要时还进行临修和检查作业。运用所一般仅配设少量存车线，一般宜采用横列式布置，如图 6–14 所示。

of stabling yard and maintenance workshop or other general layouts formed due to site conditions. For example，Osaka the Second Vehicle Depot in Japan has been gradually expanded to a special layout，and Landi High Speed EMU Depot in France is arranged by terrain conditions.

Key Point 2：Plane Layout of EMU Application and Maintenance Workshop and EMU Workshop

1. Plane Layout of EMU Application and Maintenance Workshop

EMU application and maintenance workshop is generally located at the departure station with more arrival–departure trains. It is equipped with EMU and undertakes daily inspection，temporary repair and vehicle storage. Maintenance workshop are generally equipped with 2–line daily maintenance workshop and parking lines as required. It is small in scale and generally adopts horizontal layout. It can also be designed as longitudinal layout for suitable terrain conditions.

2. Plane Layout of EMU Application Workshop

EMU application workshops are not equipped with EMUs and does not carry out daily inspection of EMU. It only undertakes vehicle storage and carries out temporary repair and inspection operation if necessary. Generally，EMU application workshops are equipped with only a few parking lines，and adopt horizontal layout，as shown in Figure 6–14.

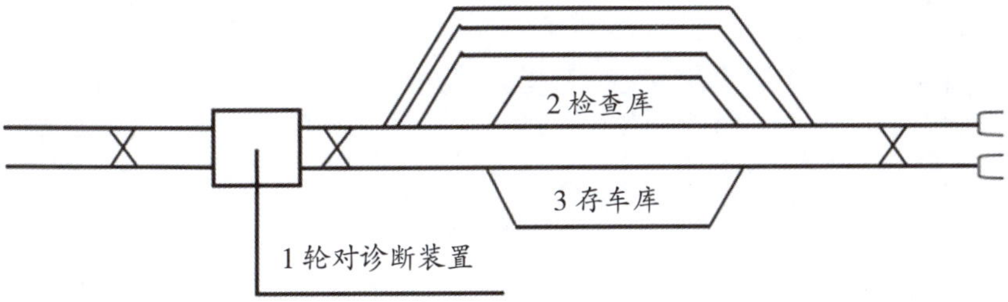

检查库 inspection workshop　存车库 parking garage　轮对诊断装置 wheelset diagnosis device

图 6-14　动车运用所横列式布置图

Figure 6-14　Horizontal Layout of EMU Workshop

知识点三：综合维修工区、大型养路机械段（工区）平面布置

综合维修管理区、大型养路机械化工务段和大型养路机械维修段的平面布置应满足作业、设备存放和维修、管理及附属设施的需要。在平面布置设计中，还应特别注意布置紧凑、减少用地。房屋等建筑物设施应尽量并栋、进行多层建设，不应在区内或段内再分专业小区，如图 6-15 所示。

Key Point 3: Plane Layout of Comprehensive Maintenance Area and Large Track Maintenance Machinery Depot（Work Section）

Layouts of comprehensive maintenance management area, large track maintenance machinery division and large track maintenance machinery depot shall meet the needs of operation, equipment storage, maintenance, management and auxiliary facilities. In layout design, special attention shall also be paid to compact layout and reduced land-use. Try to build buildings and other building facilities in parallel and multi-story. No specialized areas within depot or section, as shown in Figure 6-15.

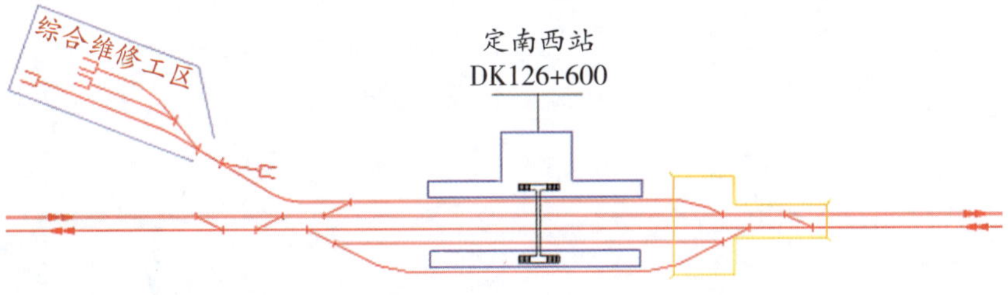

综合维修工区 comprehensive maintenance area　定南西站 Dingnan West Railway Station

图 6-15　兴业南站站台右设综合维修工区

Figure 6-15　Comprehensive Maintenance Work Section is Set up on the Right Side of Xingye South Railway Station Platform

学习笔记

Study Notes

模块三　课堂练习

搜集资料，讨论高速动车组一级、二级、三级、四级、五级检修修程及范围。

Module 3　In-class Exercises

Collect data and discuss the classification of locomotive repair and scope of Class 1，2，3，4，5 for high speed EMU.

课堂练习
In-class Exercises

模块四　课后拓展

搜集广州动车基地检修作业流程资料，分别画出三级检修作业流程图，四级、五级检修作业流程图。

Module 4　After-class Activity

Collect data of maintenance operation process in Guangzhou EMU Base and draw the Class 3 maintenance operation flow chart, the Class 4 & 5 maintenance operation flow chart, respectively.

课后拓展

After-class Activity

任务三　段、所、区与车站的布局及连接

Task 3　Layout and Connection of Depot，Workshop，Section and Station

模块一　学前准备

上网搜集高速铁路动车段、动车运用所、综合管理维修区的实物照片，并仔细观察照片上的布局情况。

Module 1　Preparation before Class

Collect online photos of high speed railway EMU depot，EMU workshop，comprehensive management and maintenance area. Observe the layout on photos carefully.

课前学习笔记
Study Notes before Class

知识点一：段、所、区与车站的布局

Key Point 1：Layout of Depot，Workshop，Section and Station

1. 高速动车段、所与车站的布置

1. Layout of High Speed EMU Depot，Workshop and Station

（1）终端式终点站与段、所成顺列布局。

（1）In-line layout of terminal station，depot and workshop.

如图 6-16 所示，终端式终点站与段、所顺列式布局能使车站咽喉区作业均衡，在一端咽喉区接发列车，在另一端咽喉区供动车车底进出动车段，两者无交叉干扰。此布局无须修建车底进出段走行线与正线的立交疏解，故工程投资也较节约。条件许可时应选用此种布局形式。

As shown in Figure 6-16，the in-line layout of terminal station，depot and workshop can make station throat operation balanced. One end of the throat receives and departures trains，at the other end of the throat，train-sets enter and exit EMU depot without cross-interference. This kind of layout does not need to build vertical untwining between running tracks of train-set entrance / exit depot and main lines，so the project investment is relatively low. This layout shall be chosen when conditions permitted.

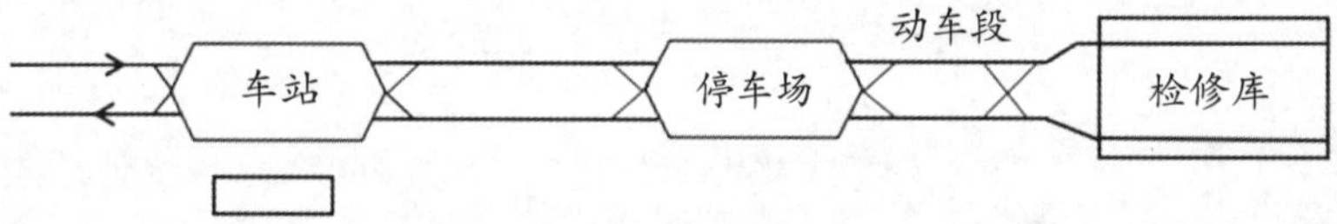

车站 station　停车场 parking yard　动车段 EMU depot　检修库 maintenance workshop

图 6-16　终端式车站与段、所成顺列布局

Figure 6-16　In-line Layout of Terminal Station，Depot and Workshop

（2）终端式终点站与段、所成反向布置。

（2）Reverse layout of terminal station，depot and workshop.

终端式车站与段、所成反向布置，如图 6-17 所示。当车站位于市区或顺车站方向的延伸地带，处于密集的市内甚至是城市中心地区，无法采用顺列式布局。

Reverse layout of terminal station，depot and workshop is shown in Figure 6-17，the station is located in urban area or along the extension zone in a dense city or even a city center，the in-line layout cannot be adopted.

Disadvantages of this layout：both

这种布置的缺点：列车到发和车底进出段都在一端咽喉区，造成咽喉能力紧张且一部分到发列车和车底进出段必然产生平面交叉。

arrival–departure trains and train–sets entrance / exit depot are located at one end of the throat, which causing tension in throat capacity. Some arrival–departure trains and train–set entrance / exit depot will inevitably result in level–crossing.

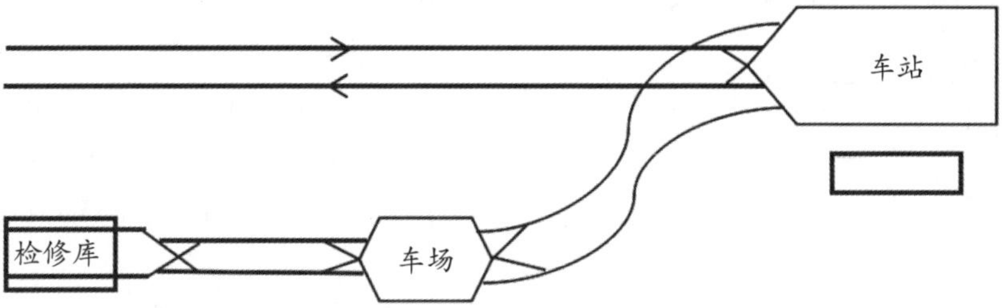

车站 station　车场 train yard　检修库 maintenance workshop

图 6–17　京沪高铁徐州—上海段设计的段、所、区分布示意图

Figure 6–17　Schematic Figure of Layout of Depot, Workshop and Section Designed for Xuzhou–Shanghai Section of Beijing–Shanghai High Speed Railway

（3）贯通式车站与段、所的顺列布置。

如图 6–18，贯通式车站与运用维修所的顺列布局是常用的形式，京沪高铁的济南、徐州、南京等站的运用维修所均属此种布局。

(3) In–line layout of through–type station, depot and workshop.

As shown in Figure 6–18, the in–line layout of through–type station and operation maintenance workshop is a commonly used form. Operation maintenance workshops of Jinan, Xuzhou, Nanjing, etc. on Beijing–Shanghai High Speed Railway Line all belong to this kind of layout.

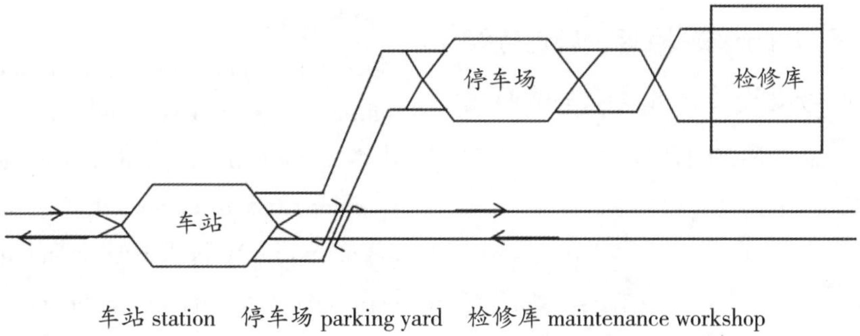

车站 station　停车场 parking yard　检修库 maintenance workshop

图 6–18　京沪高铁贯通式车站与段、所的顺列分布示意图

Figure 6–18　Schematic Figure of In–Line Layout of Through–Type Station, Depot and Workshop of Beijing–Shanghai High Speed Railway

（4）贯通式车站与段、所的并列或斜并列布置多为规模较小的动车运用所与车站所采用，如京沪线的蚌埠站。

（5）正线外包段、所与车站纵列的布局。

此布局使用方便。但高速铁路线路技术标准很高，一般难以作出这种布置，如图 6-19 所示。

（4）Parallel or inclined parallel layout of through-type station，depot and workshop is the mostly used layout for small-scale operation workshop and station，e.g. Bengbu Station on Beijing Shanghai High Speed Railway Line.

（5）Longitudinal layout of main line outsourcing depot，workshop and station.

This kind of layout is convenient to use. But the technical standards for high speed line are very high and it is difficult to make such an arrangement，as shown in Figure 6-19.

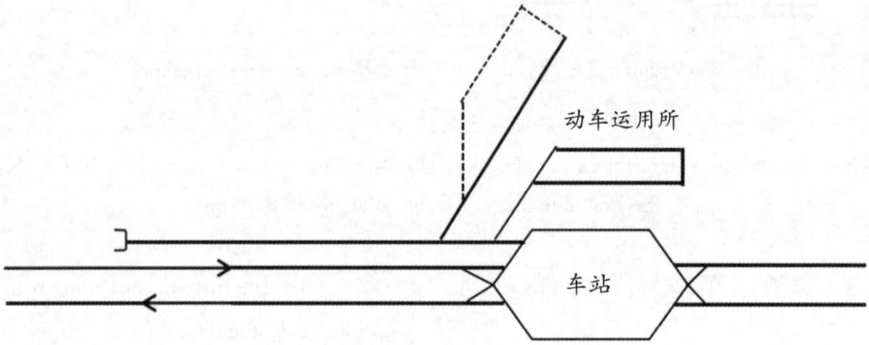

动车运用所 EMU workshop　车站 station

图 6-19　正线外包段、所与车站纵列的布局

Figure 6-19　Longitudinal Layout of Main Line Outsourcing Depot，Workshop and Station

2. 综合维修管理区与车站的布局

（1）综合维修管理区所需面积较大，应尽量布置于车站附近，以走行线与车站在咽喉处连接，可设于车站两端任何象限，如图 6-20 所示。

2. Layout of Comprehensive Maintenance and Management Area and Station

（1）Comprehensive maintenance and management area is widely distributed，it shall be located near station as far as possible. Running track is connected with station at the throat and it can be located in any quadrant at both ends of station，as shown in Figure 6-20.

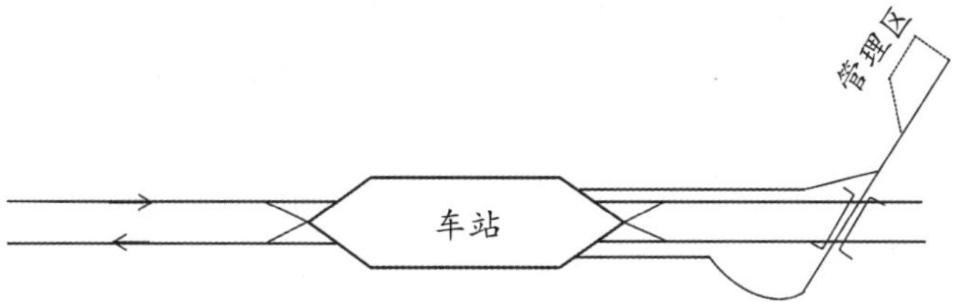

车站 station　管理区 management area

图 6–20　综合维修管理区设在车站附近，以走行线与车站在咽喉处连接
Figure 6–20　Comprehensive Maintenance and Management Area is Located Near Station，Running Track is Connected with Station at the Throat

（2）若设于车站附近引起造价大增时，管理区也可设在区间，从正线出岔衔接，如图 6–21 所示。如京沪高速铁路在常州和无锡站间设的浒墅关管理区。

（2）If the construction cost will increase greatly near station，the management area can be set in section and connected with main line，as shown in Figure 6–21. For example，Hushuguan Management Area is set in the section between Changzhou Station and Wuxi Station on Beijing–Shanghai High Speed Railway.

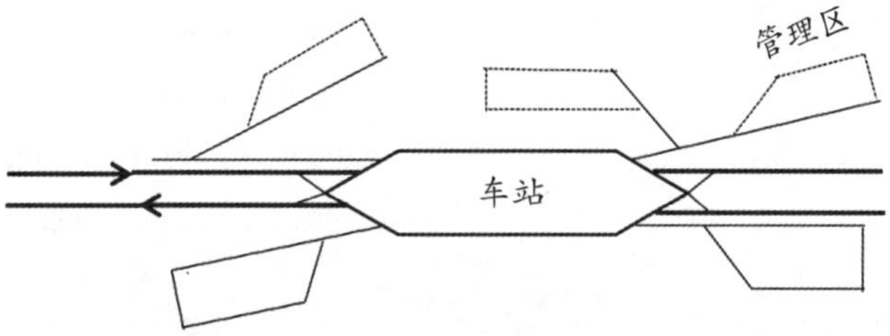

车站 station　管理区 management area

图 6–21　管理区也可设在区间，从正线出岔衔接
Figure 6–21　Management Area can be Set in Section to Connect with Main Line

（3）管理区应尽量与工务段，动车段、所等设在一处，以共用走行线和减少用地。

（3）Management area shall be located at the same place with maintenance division，EMU depot and workshop，etc. They can share running track and reduce land–use.

知识点二：段、所、区与车站的连接

（1）综合维修管理区分布广、数量多，并要求与车站或正线有便捷的通路连接，如图 6-20 所示。

（2）动车段、所与车站连接。

① 动车段与车站间的走行线尽量布置在正线两侧，其中一条以立交穿越正线，这样可有效减少到发线与车底走行在咽喉区的交叉干扰。

② 动车运用维修所和动车运用所因始发终到高速列车较少，且发车和收车与通过列车时间往往错开，咽喉区交叉少。

Key Point 2：Connection between Depot，Workshop，Section and Station

（1）Comprehensive maintenance and management area is widely distributed with a large number. It requires convenient access road to station or main line，as shown in Figure 6-20.

（2）Connection between EMU depot，workshop and station.

① Running tracks between EMU depot and station shall be set on both sides of the main line. One of them shall pass through main line by interchange. It can effectively reduce cross-interference between receiving-departure line and train-set running in throat area.

② There are fewer arrival-departure high speed trains at EMU operation and maintenance workshops and EMU workshops. Train departure and arrived times are often staggered by train passing time，so that there are fewer throat crossings.

学习笔记

Study Notes

模块三　课堂练习

讨论高速铁路动车段、所与车站的布局造成的优势和劣势。

Module 3　In-class Exercises

Discuss advantages and disadvantages of the layout of EMU depot, workshop and station for high speed railway.

课堂练习

In-class Exercises

模块四　课后拓展

打开手机地图，寻找离你最近的高速铁路动车段、所、区，并分析段、所、区与车站的布局情况。

Module 4　After-class Activity

Open the Map on your mobile phone, and locate the high speed railway EMU depot, workshop and section nearest to you. Analyze the layout of its depot, workshop, section and station.

课后拓展

After-class Activity

项目七　高速铁路引入大城市铁路枢纽设计

Project 7　Design for Introducing High Speed Railway into Railway Terminal in Metropolis

任务一　利用枢纽内既有铁路及车站的技术要求

Task 1　Technical Requirements of Using Existing Railway and Station in Railway Terminal

模块一　学前准备

查找一个由既有站改造的可乘坐高铁的铁路车站，将车站照片打印并粘贴在下方，同时简述该车站规模、线路、站台等基本情况。

Module 1　Preparation before Class

Find a railway station which is reconstructed of the existing station and can carry bullet train. Print and paste the station photo below, and briefly describe the basic situation of station scale, field of lines, and platform, etc.

课前学习笔记
Study Notes before Class

模块二　课堂学习

Module 2　In-class Learning

知识点一：铁路枢纽

Key Point 1：Railway Terminal

1. 铁路枢纽的定义

1. Definition of Railway Terminal

铁路枢纽指在两条以上铁路干支线的交会处或终端地区，由一个或几个统一调度协调作业的专业站（包括客运站、货运站、编组站）以及相应的正线、进出站线、联络线、迂回线、环线等铁路设备组成的整体。

Railway terminal refers to the meeting point or terminal area of more than two railway trunk lines and branch lines. It is a whole that includes one or several professional stations (including passenger station, freight station, marshalling station) under unified management and relevant railway equipment such as main line, station approach track, connecting line, detour line, loop line, etc.

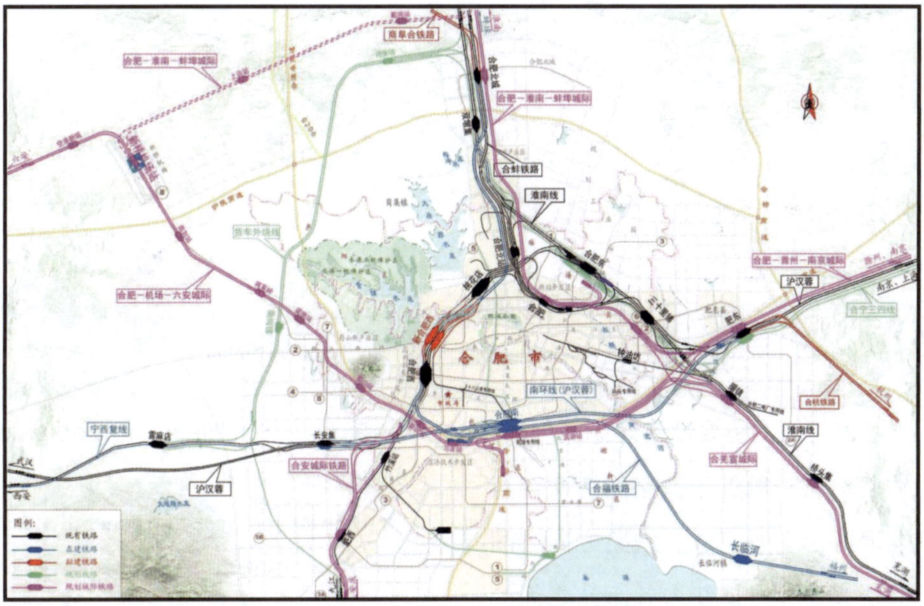

图 7-1　合肥铁路枢纽规划总布置图

Figure 7-1　General Layout of Hefei Railway Terminal Planning

以合肥铁路枢纽规划为例，根据中国铁路总公司和安徽省人民政府《关于合肥铁路枢纽规划（2016—2030年）的批复》，合肥铁路枢纽主要由合肥站、合肥南站和新合肥西站三大主站和一个辅助的既有站合肥西站（待新合肥西站建成后改名）组成。

Taking Hefei Railway Terminal Planning as an example, according to CHINA RAILWAY (CR) and the People's Government of Anhui Province on the Approval of Hefei Railway Terminal Planning (2016–2030), Hefei railway terminal is mainly composed of three main stations as Hefei Railway Station, Hefei South Railway Station, New Hefei West Railway Station and an auxiliary existing station, i.e Hefei West Railway Station (renamed after the completion of New Hefei West Railway Station).

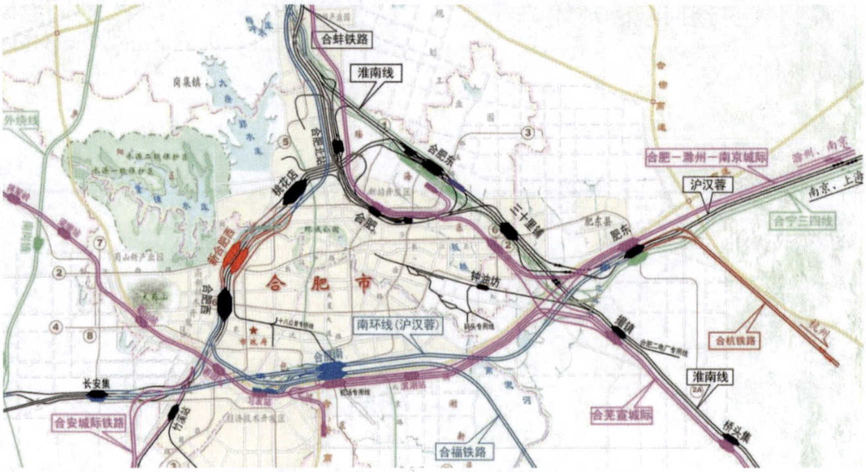

图 7-2　合肥铁路枢纽车站位置图

Figure 7-2　Location of Hefei Railway Terminal Station

2. 铁路枢纽的主要设施设备

铁路枢纽一般处于铁路网的交会点或终端地区，主要完成各铁路方向之间列车的转线作业、枢纽内各车站之间的车流交换、旅客换乘与货物运输组织等作业。因此，铁路枢纽包含下列设备：

2. Main Facilities and Equipment of Railway Terminal

Railway terminals are generally located at the meeting points or terminal areas of railway network, mainly include train shunting operation of different railway directions, traffic flow exchange between stations in terminal, passenger transfer, freight transport organization, etc.Therefore, railway terminal contains the following equipment:

（1）铁路线路。

铁路线路包括引入正线、到发线、联络线、环线、调车线、迂回线、工业企业线等。

（1）Railway line.

It includes lead-in main line，receiving-departure track，connecting line，loop line，shunting track，detour line，industrial enterprise line，etc.

图 7-3 昆明站至昆明南站联络线

Figure 7-3 Connecting Line between Kunming Railway Station and Kunming South Railway Station

（2）车站。

车站包括客运站、编组站、中间站、货运站（铁路物流中心）、工业站、港湾站等。

（2）Station.

It includes passenger station，marshalling station，intermediate station，freight station （railway logistics center），industrial station，harbor station，etc.

图 7-4 福州南站

Figure 7-4 Fuzhou South Railway Station

（3）疏解设备。

疏解设备包括铁路线路与铁路线路的平面和立交疏解、铁路线路与城市公路的跨线桥和平交道口以及线路所等。

（3）Untwining facilities.

It includes plane and vertical untwining of railway lines，cross-line bridge and level crossing of railway line and urban road，and block house.

图 7-5　上海火车站恒丰路立交桥

Figure 7-5　Hengfeng Road Interchange of Shanghai Railway Station

（4）其他设备。

其他设备指的是运输服务的有关设备组成的总体，包括机务段、车辆段、客车整备所等。

（4）Other facilities.

The overall composition of relevant equipment for transport service，including locomotive depot，car depot，passenger car servicing post，etc.

图 7-6　北京机务段

Figure 7-6　Beijing Locomotive Depot

3. 铁路枢纽的分类

（1）按其在铁路网上的地位和作用分类。

①路网性铁路枢纽承担的客货运量和车流组织任务涉及整个铁路网。这类枢纽一般位于几条铁路干线交叉或衔接处的大城市，办理大量的跨局通过车流和地方车流，设有较多的专业车站，其设备和规模能力都很大。

②区域性铁路枢纽承担的客货运量和车流组织主要为一定的区域范围服务。枢纽一般位于干线和支线的交叉或衔接处的大中型城市，办理所管辖的通过车流和地方车流，设备规模不大。

③地方性铁路枢纽承担的客货运量和车流组织主要为某一工业区或港湾等地方作业服务。枢纽一般位于大工业企业和水陆联运地区，办理大量的货物装卸和小量运转服务作业。

（2）按专业车站和铁路线路在枢纽布置图上的结构特点分类。

①一站铁路枢纽：由一个综合性车站和 3 条或 4 条引入线组成，通常位于中小型城市。

3. Classification of Railway Terminal

(1) Classification by position and function in railway network.

① Network railway terminal undertaken passenger and freight volume, and traffic flow organization task are involved in the terminal of entire railway network. The terminal is generally located in a large city where several trunk lines cross or connect. It deals with a large number of crossing traffic flow and local traffic flow. There are many professional stations in the terminal with large equipment, scale and capacity.

② Regional railway terminal: The undertaken passenger and freight volume, and traffic flow organization mainly serve for a certain region. The terminal is generally located in large and medium-sized cities where trunk lines and branch lines cross or connect. It deals with passing traffic flow and local traffic flow; the equipment and scale is not large.

③ Local railway terminal: The undertaken traffic volume and traffic flow organization are mainly for serving certain industrial area or harbors operation.Generally, the terminal is located in large industrial enterprise and land-water combined transport area and it deals with a large number of goods loading and unloading and small transfer service operation.

(2) Classification by professional station and structural characteristics of railway line in terminal layout.

① Terminal with one station: It consists of a comprehensive station and 3 or 4 lead-in lines, usually located in small and medium-sized cities.

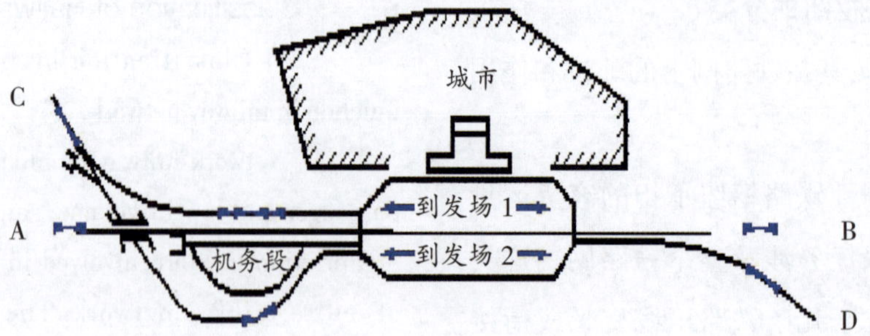

城市 city　机务段 locomotive depot　到发场 receiving-departure yard

图 7-7　一站铁路枢纽布局图

Figure 7-7　Layout of Terminal with One Station

②三角形铁路枢纽：引入枢纽线汇集于三点，并在三点间修建相应的联络线，适用于各个方向客货流量都有较大转换的情形。

② Triangle railway terminal: lead-in hub lines are assembled at three points, and relevant connecting lines are built between the three points, which is suitable for large transfer of passenger and freight flows in all directions.

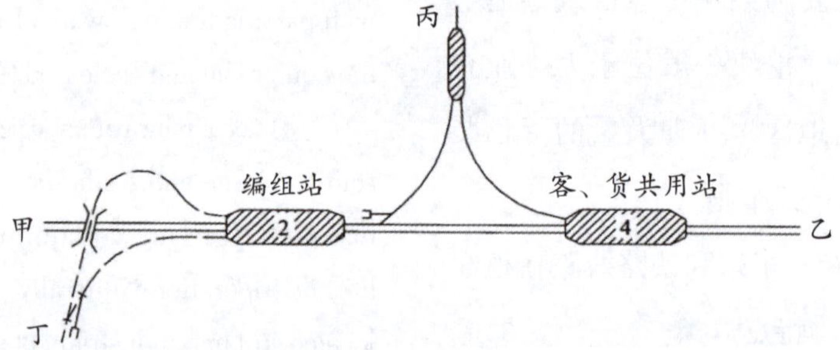

编组站 marshalling station　客、货共用站 mixed passenger and freight station

甲 first　乙 second　丙 third　丁 fourth

图 7-8　三角形铁路枢纽布局图

Figure 7-8　Layout of Triangle Railway Terminal

③十字形铁路枢纽：两条铁路线路近似正交，在枢纽中心设有呈十字形的交叉疏解布置，适用于直行流量大、转向流量小的枢纽布局。

③ Cross-type railway terminal: two railway lines are approximately orthogonal. Cross-type crossing untwining is set in terminal center, which is suitable for terminal layout with large straight flow and small turning flow.

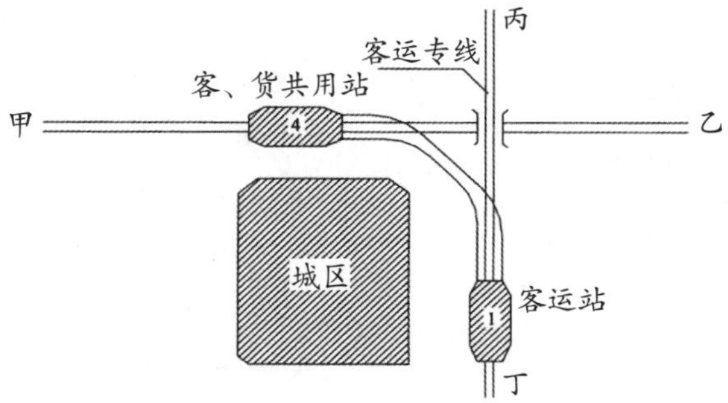

客运站 passenger station　城区 urban area　客、货共用站 mixed passenger and freight station
客运专线 passenger dedicated line　甲 first　乙 second　丙 third　丁 fourth

图 7-9　十字形铁路枢纽布局图
Figure 7-9　Cross-Type Railway Terminal

④顺列式铁路枢纽：枢纽内所有车站（客运站、货运站、技术作业站等）都按顺序纵列布置在枢纽内同一条伸长的通道上（受地形影响，不得不如此布局）。

④ In-line railway terminal: all stations (passenger station, freight station, technical operation station, etc.) in terminal are arranged in line on the same extended access road (arranged by terrain condition).

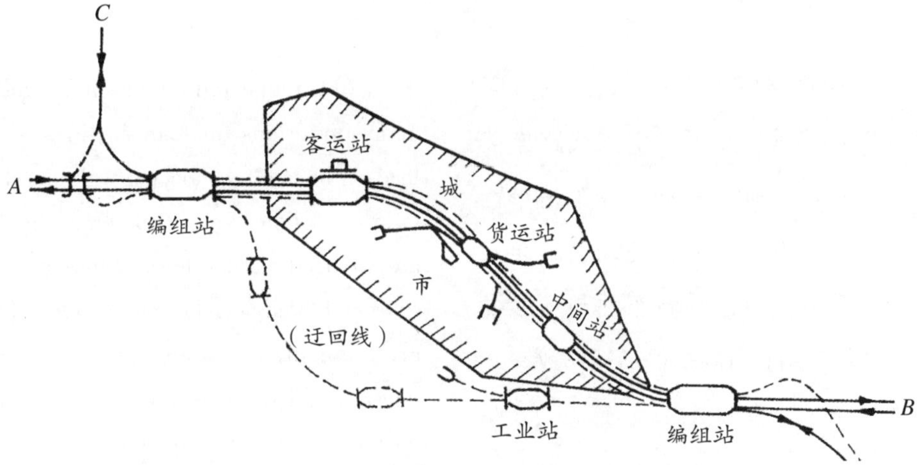

编组站 marshalling station　客运站 passenger station　货运站 freight station
中间站 intermediate station　迂回线 detour line　工业站 industrial station　城市 city

图 7-10　顺列式铁路枢纽布局图
Figure 7-10　Layout of In-Line Railway Terminal

⑤并列式铁路枢纽：编组站与客运站平行布置，衔接铁路线路，先按线路方向引入枢纽，然后列车按种类分别引入平行布置的编组站和客运站等。

⑤ Parallel arrangement type railway terminal：marshalling station and passenger station are arranged in parallel.Connecting railway lines are firstly introduced into terminal by route direction，and then trains are introduced to parallel marshalling station and passenger station respectively based on their types.

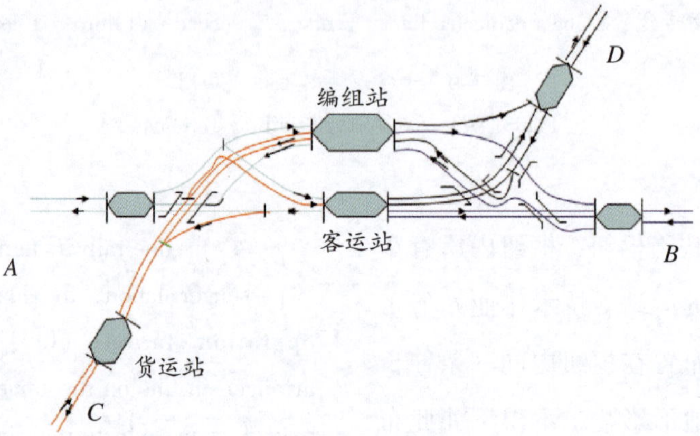

编组站 marshalling station　客运站 passenger station　货运站 freight station

图 7-11　并列式铁路枢纽布局图

Figure 7-11　Layout of Parallel Arrangement Type Railway Terminal

⑥环形铁路枢纽：引入线路的方向较多，以环形线路将所有引入线路连接起来形成一个整体。各种专业车站布置在环线、半环线上，或自环线引出伸入城市中心附近，联络线将车站与环形线路连接，其作用和目的是提高运作效率，方便调度、运转等作业。

⑥ Circular railway terminal：there are many directions for lead-in lines，and all lead-in lines are connected with circular line to form a whole. Various professional stations are arranged on loop line，semi-circular line or extend to city center from loop line. Stations are connected to loop line by connecting lines，with its function and purpose to improve operation efficiency and facilitate dispatch and transfer operation.

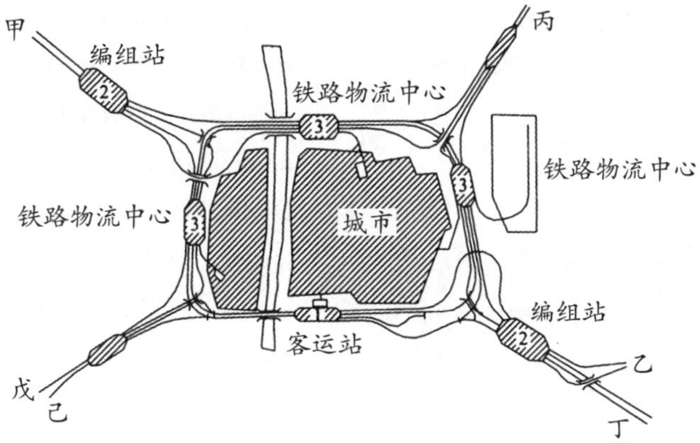

1- 客运站 passenger station 2- 编组站 marshalling station 3- 铁路物流中心 railway logistics center
城市 city 甲 first 乙 second 丙 third 丁 fourth 戊 fifth 己 sixth

图 7-12 环形铁路枢纽布局图
Figure 7-12 Layout of Circular Railway Terminal

⑦尽端式铁路枢纽：位于铁路路网的终点或起点，一般设在大港湾、大工业园或采矿区等有大宗资源产生或消失的地区。

⑦ Dead-end railway terminal: it is located at starting point or ending point of railway network and generally set in areas where large amount of resources is generated or disappeared, e.g. big harbor, big industrial park or mining area.

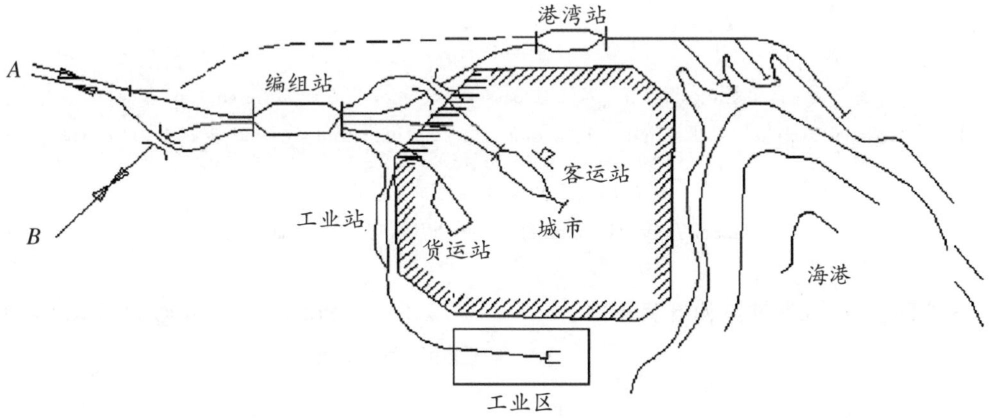

编组站 marshalling station 客运站 passenger station 货运站 freight station
港湾站 harbor station 工业站 industrial station 工业区 industrial area 城市 city 海港 harbor

图 7-13 尽端式铁路枢纽布置图
Figure 7-13 Layout of Dead-End Railway Terminal

⑧组合式铁路枢纽：受路网发展、城市改建、车流条件、自然条件等多因素影响，当单一类型枢纽布置已无法满足运营需要时，可以将枢纽设计成与枢纽所担负的作业量和作业性质相适应的由几种类型枢纽组合而成的组合式枢纽。

⑧ Combined railway terminal：due to the influence of road network development，urban reconstruction，traffic flow condition，natural condition，etc.，when a single type of terminal layout can no longer meet its operation needs，it can be designed as a combined railway terminal composed of several types of terminals，which is suitable for the operation volume and operation nature undertaken by terminal.

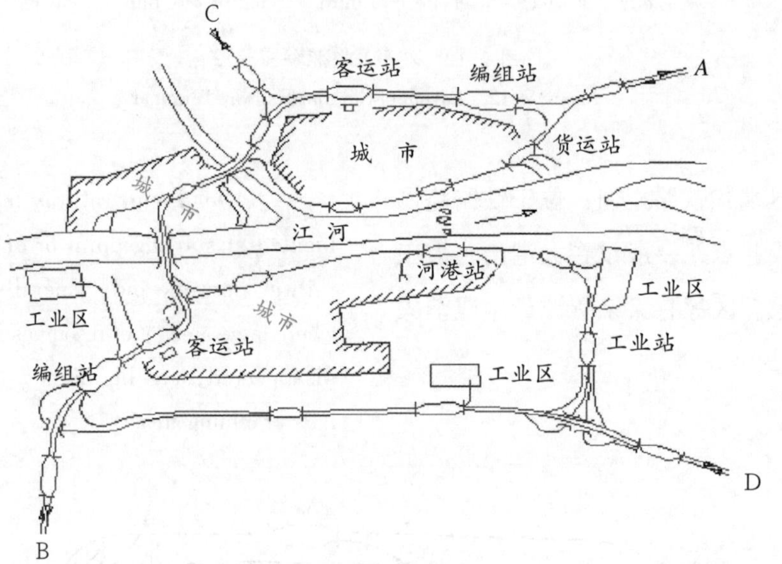

编组站 marshalling station　客运站 passenger station　货运站 freight station
河港站 river port station　工业站 industrial station　工业区 industrial area　城市 city　江河 rivers

图 7-14　组合式铁路枢纽布局图

Figure 7-14　Layout of Combined Railway Terminal

知识点二：既有铁路和既有车站

Key Point 2：Existing Railway and Existing Station

1. 既有铁路

既有铁路就是指已经建成通车的铁路，区别于新建、在建、规划中的铁路。

既有线改造是指对既有铁路线路进行改造，通常包括既有线施工作业和维

1. Existing Railway

Existing Railway refers to the railway that has been completed and opened to traffic，which is different from the newly-built，being-built and planned railway.

修作业两大方面的内容。

（1）既有线施工作业的内容。

①线路及站场设备技术改造，增建双线、新线引入、电气化改造等施工。

Reconstruct existing railway line refers to the reconstruction of existing railway line, which usually consists of construction work and maintenance operation of existing railway line.

(1) Construction work of existing line.

① Equipment and technique improvement of line, station and yard, construction of double lines, introduction of new line, and electrification transformation, etc.

图 7-15　渝黔铁路既有线施工

Figure 7-15　Construction Work at Existing Chongqing-Guizhou Railway Line

②跨越、穿越线路和站场，架设桥梁、人行过道，铺设管道、渡槽和电力线路、通信线路、油气管线等设施的施工。

② Cross or pass through line, station and yard, build bridge and foot-crossing, lay pipeline, aqueduct, power cable, communication line, oil gas pipeline and other facilities.

图 7-16 转体斜拉桥跨越京广铁路（河北省保定市乐凯大街南延工程）

Figure 7-16 Swivel Cable-Stayed Bridge Crossing Beijing-Guangzhou Railway（Nanyan Project of Lekai Avenue in Baoding City，Hebei Province）

③在线路安全保护区内架设、铺设管道、渡槽和电力线路、通信线路、油气管线等设施的施工。

④在规定的安全区域内实施爆破作业，线路隐蔽工程（含通信、信号、电力电缆径路）作业，影响路基稳定的各种施工。

⑤在信号、联锁、闭塞、CTC/TDCS、列控、通信等行车设备上的大中修施工作业。

⑥线路大中修，路基、桥隧大修及大型养路机械施工作业，接触网大修作业。

（2）既有线维修作业的内容。

维修作业应利用维修天窗进行，作业开始前不须限速，结束后须达到正常放行列车条件。

③ Erect and lay pipeline，aqueduct，power cable，communication line，oil gas pipeline and other facilities in line safety protection zone.

④ Blasting operations shall be carried out within specified safe area. Operations carried out on concealed works of lines（including communication，signal and power cable route）. Various construction work affects the stability of earthwork.

⑤ Major and medium repair and construction operation on signal，interlocking，blocking，CTC/TDCS，train control，communication and other running equipment.

⑥ Major and medium repair of lines，overhaul of earthwork，bridge and tunnel，large track maintenance machinery construction operation and overhaul of overhead contact system.

（2）Maintenance work of existing line.

Maintenance operation shall be carried

out through maintaining skylight. No speed limit is required before operation starts, and normal train release conditions shall be reached after operation ends.

2. 既有车站

既有车站是指铁路线路规划时已建成使用的车站，区别于新建、在建、规划中的车站。例如，北京南站在京沪高铁开通前已是京津城际铁路的始发站，此时的北京南站就是既有车站；京沪高铁在途经安徽蚌埠设立的蚌埠南站，就不是既有车站，而是新建车站。

2. Existing Station

Existing station refers to the station that has been completed and used in railway line planning, which is different from the newly-built, being-built and planned station. For example, Beijing South Railway Station was the departure station of Beijing-Tianjin Intercity Railway before Beijing-Shanghai High Speed Railway was opened. Therefore, Beijing South Railway Station is an existing station. But Bengbu South Railway Station set up in Bengbu, Anhui Province and of Beijing-Shanghai High Speed Railway is not an existing station, but a newly-built station.

图 7-17 京沪高铁蚌埠南站

Figure 7-17 Bengbu South Railway Station of Beijing-Shanghai High Speed Railway

知识点三：高速铁路引入既有枢纽的要求

高速铁路的起讫点和经由点多数位于既有大城市的铁路枢纽，因此，高速铁路引入既有枢纽应满足以下要求：

（1）高速铁路的走向要与城市规划和铁路枢纽总布置图密切配合。

（2）铁路枢纽内客运系统要与货运系统密切配合。

（3）铁路枢纽内高速铁路车站要与其他客运站密切配合。

（4）高速铁路要与近、远期规划引入铁路枢纽的新线密切配合。

Key Point 3: Requirements of Introducing High Speed Railway into Existing Terminal

The starting/ending points and transit points of high speed railway are mostly located in existing railway terminals of large cities. Therefore, introducing high speed railway into existing terminal shall meet the following requirements:

（1）The trend of high speed railway should be closely coordinated with city overall planning and general layout of railway terminal.

（2）Passenger transport system should closely cooperate with freight transport system in railway terminal.

（3）High speed railway station should closely cooperate with other passenger stations in railway terminal.

（4）High speed railway should closely cooperate with new lines which are to be introduced into the railway terminal in short and long-term planning.

知识点四：高速铁路引入既有枢纽的方式

（1）根据引入线的平、纵断面不同，可以将引入方式分为三类：平面引入、高架引入、地下引入。

（2）根据引入客运站的类别，可以将引入方式分为两类：引入既有站（合设方案）、引入新建站（分设方案）。

（3）根据高速铁路线路走向和既有线的关系，引入方式可以分为三类：并

Key Point 4: Ways of Introducing High Speed Railway into Existing Terminal

（1）According to different plane and profile of lead-in lines, it can be divided into three types: plane introduction, elevated introduction and underground introduction.

（2）According to passenger station types to be introduced, it can be divided into two types: introduction of existing station（combined scheme）and introduction of newly-built station（separate scheme）.

行引入、并线引入、分线引入。

①并行引入方式。

优势：并行引入方式对城市不产生重新分割；站房共用，便于旅客换乘；可充分利用既有客运设施和市政公用设施。

劣势：高速铁路线路穿越市区与城市干道交叉，拆迁工程量较大，高速铁路线路在枢纽内的技术条件受到一定限制，将会影响高速列车在枢纽内的运行速度。

(3) According to relationship between the trend of high speed railway line and existing line, it can be divided into three types: parallel introduction, combined introduction and distributing introduction.

① Parallel introduction.

Advantages: parallel introduction does not re-divide city; station and yard are shared for passenger's transfer convenience; existing passenger transport facilities and municipal public utilities can be fully used.

Disadvantages: high speed railway lines pass through urban area and cross with city trunk road, so the demolition work is relatively large. Technical conditions of high speed railway line in terminal are limited to a certain extent, which will affect the running speed of high speed train in terminal.

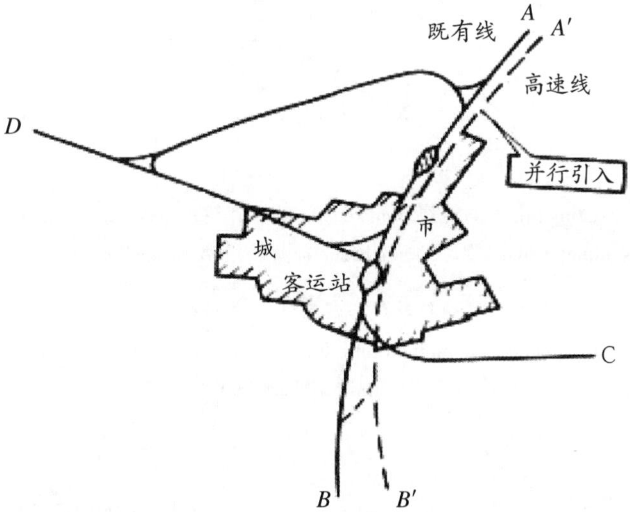

既有线 existing line　高速线 high speed line　客运站 passenger station　城市 city
并行引入 parallel introduction

图 7-18　高速铁路线路与既有线并行引入铁路枢纽示意图

Figure 7-18　Schematic Figure of Parallel Introduction of High Speed Railway Line and Existing Line into Railway Terminal

②并线引入方式。

优势：并线引入方式工程量小，节约城市用地，拆迁工程量也少，高速线路对城市干扰小。

劣势：高速列车在枢纽内的合并区间需减速运行，且由于该区间客、货混跑，通过能力紧张，必须修建四线或多线方能满足需要。

② Combined introduction.

Advantages: combined introduction has small quantities of work, saves urban land, and reduces demolition work. High speed line has little interference to the city.

Disadvantages: high speed train in combined section of terminal area needs to run at a reduced speed. Due to mixed running of passenger and freight transport in this section, the carrying capacity is tight. Four or more lines must be built to meet the needs.

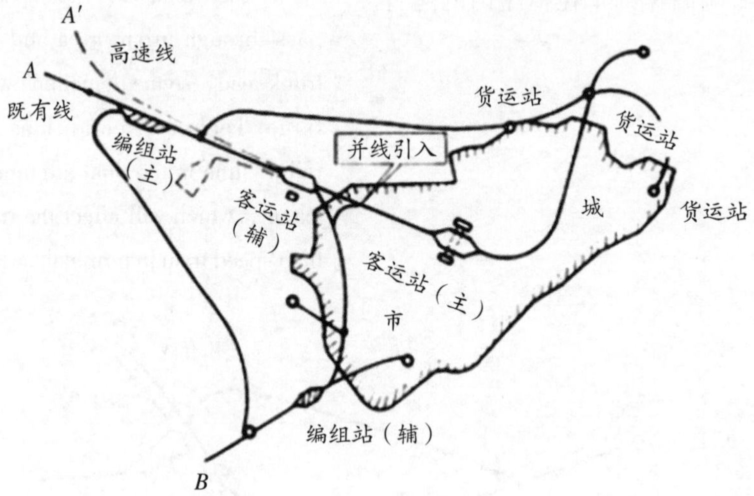

既有线 existing line　高速线 high speed line　客运站 passenger station　城市 city
并线引入 combined introduction　货运站 freight station　编组站 marshalling station　主 major　辅 auxiliary

图 7–19　高速铁路线与既有线并线引入铁路枢纽示意图

Figure 7–19　Schematic Figure of Combined Introduction of High Speed Railway Line and Existing Line into Railway Terminal

③分线引入方式。

优势：分线引入方式对城市环境影响少，拆迁工程量小，有利于扩大枢纽的客运能力，高速线路的施工不影响运营。

③ Distributing introduction.

Advantages: distributing introduction has less impact on urban environment with less demolition work, which is conducive to expanding terminal passenger capacity. Train operation will not be affected by the construction work of high speed line.

劣势：新建高速站远离城市中心，不利于吸引客流，且与既有主要客运站相隔甚远，不利于旅客换乘。

Disadvantages: the newly-built high speed station is far away from city center, which is not conducive to attracting passenger flow. And it is also far away from the major existing passenger station, which is not convenient for passenger transfer.

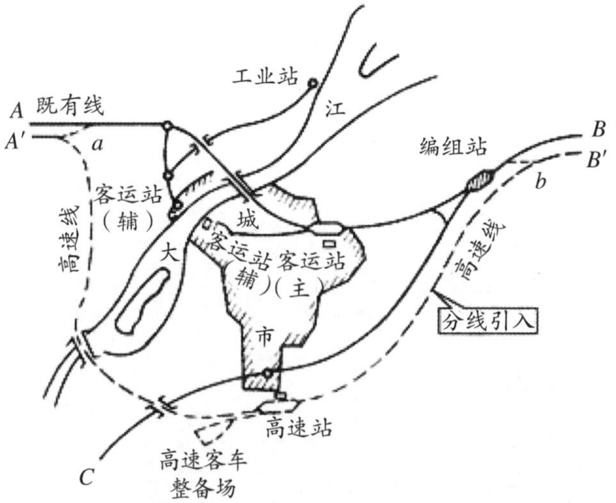

既有线 existing line　高速线 high speed line　客运站 passenger station　城市 city
分线引入 distributing introduction　高速站 high speed station　编组站 marshalling station　主 major
辅 auxiliary　大江 river　工业站 industrial station　高速客车整备场 high speed passenger car servicing yard

图 7-20　高速铁路线路与既有线分线引入铁路枢纽示意图

Figure 7-20　Schematic Figure of Distributing Introduction of High Speed Railway Line and Existing Line into Railway Terminal

学习笔记

Study Notes

模块三 课堂练习

问题 1：查阅资料，沪昆高铁云南段和云桂铁路云南段哪些车站是新建车站，哪些是既有车站？

问题 2：查阅资料，高速铁路主要采用哪种方式引入昆明铁路枢纽，请列举说明。

Module 3 In-class Exercises

Question 1: Do research and find out the newly-built stations and existing stations in Yunnan section of Shanghai-Kunming High Speed Railway, as well as Yunnan section of Yunnan-Guangxi Railway.

Question 2: Do research and make explanations about the main way of introducing high speed railway into Kunming Railway Terminal.

课堂练习

In-class Exercises

模块四　课后拓展

Module 4　After-class Activity

简析南昌铁路枢纽的定位、组成部分及其车站功能。

Make a brief analysis of the positioning, components and station function of Nanchang Railway Terminal.

课后拓展

After-class Activity

任务二　高速铁路通过铁路枢纽的设计要求

Task 2　Design Requirements for High Speed Railway Passing through Railway Terminal

模块一　学前准备

查阅资料，请在《中长期铁路网规划（2016—2030）》确定的铁路枢纽中，列举任意一个铁路枢纽的所有线路，包括已建成线路、在建线路和规划线路。

Module 1　Preparation before Class

Do research and choose one railway terminal determined in the Medium and Long-Term Railway Network Planning（2016-2030）to list all railway lines in it，including built，being-built and planned lines in the railway terminal.

课前学习笔记

Study Notes before Class

模块二　课堂学习

知识点一：高速铁路通过铁路枢纽的设计要求

1. 与铁路枢纽总图规划相适应

（1）符合铁路网规划和铁路枢纽总图规划。对于铁路枢纽总图格局尚未形成或总图规划尚未有定论的铁路枢纽，需要与枢纽总图规划同步研究高速铁路引入或通过问题。

（2）综合考虑高速铁路线路与既有客运站的分布、分工，高速铁路线路引入（通过）的具体位置走向，高速动车段、区、所等设施的位置方案等问题。

2. 与城市规划发展相适应

（1）符合城市总体规划，结合地形地质条件，减少拆迁工程，做到布局合理。

（2）符合城市综合交通规划，处理好高速铁路与其他交通方式的衔接问题，吸引客流，方便旅客出行。

Module 2　In-class Learning

Key Point 1：Design Requirements for High Speed Railway Passing through Railway Terminal

1. Adapt to the General Planning of Railway Terminal

（1）Conform to railway network planning and general planning of railway terminal. For railway terminal whose general layout has not been formed or general planning has not been finalized，it is necessary to study the introduction or passing of high speed railway with general layout planning simultaneously.

（2）Comprehensive consideration shall be given to distribution of high speed railway line and existing passenger station，their division of labor，specific location and trend of introducing （passing） of high speed railway line，and location schemes of high speed EMU depot，section，workshop and other facilities，etc.

2. Adapt to the Development of City Overall Planning

（1）Conform to city overall planning，combine with terrain and geological conditions，reduce demolition work and make a reasonable layout.

（2）Conform to urban comprehensive transportation planning，properly handle the connection of high speed railway and other modes of transportation，attract passenger flow，facilitate passenger travel.

3. 高速铁路线路的设计要求与技术标准

铁路线路设计应落实现代综合交通运输发展要求、准确把握项目功能定位等总体要求。

铁路线路设计的主要技术标准、综合选线、线路平面、线路纵断面、车站分布等主要内容须符合《铁路线路设计规范》（TB 10098—2017）、《高速铁路设计规范》（TB 10621—2014）的规定。

3. Design Requirements and Technical Standards of High Speed Railway Line

The design of railway line shall implement the overall requirements of modern comprehensive transportation development and grasp project functional orientation accurately.

Main technical standards for railway line design, comprehensive route selection, line plane, line profile, distribution of station and other main contents shall comply with the provisions of "Code for Design of Railway Line "（TB 10098-2017）and "Code for Design of High Speed Railway"（TB 10621-2014）.

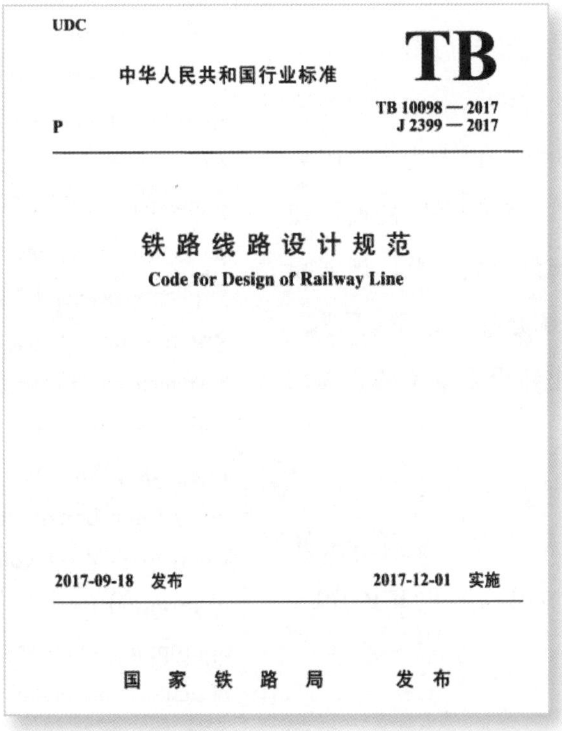
UDC

中华人民共和国行业标准 TB

P

TB 10098 — 2017
J 2399 — 2017

铁 路 线 路 设 计 规 范
Code for Design of Railway Line

2017-09-18 发布 2017-12-01 实施

国 家 铁 路 局 发 布

图 7-21 行业标准《铁路线路设计规范》（TB 10098—2017）
Figure 7-21 Industry Standard "Code for Design of Railway Line"（TB 10098-2017）

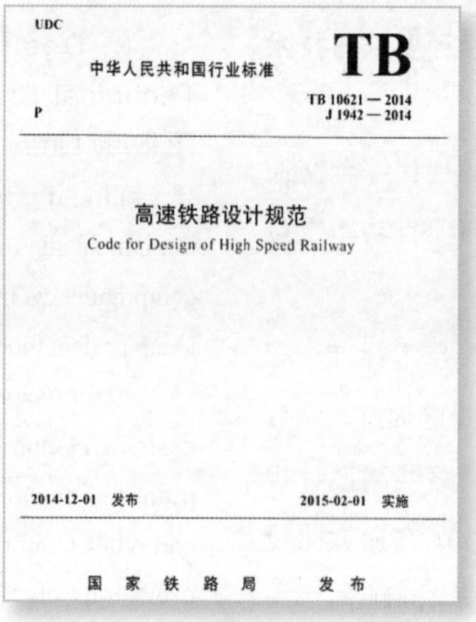

UDC

中华人民共和国行业标准

TB

P

TB 10621 — 2014
J 1942 — 2014

高速铁路设计规范

Code for Design of High Speed Railway

2014-12-01 发布

2015-02-01 实施

国 家 铁 路 局 发 布

图 7-22 行业标准《高速铁路设计规范》（TB 10621—2014）

Figure 7-22 Industry Standard "Code for Design of High Speed Railway" （TB 10621-2014）

4. 铁路车站及枢纽的设计要求与技术标准

铁路车站及枢纽设计应全面落实生态环境保护、水土保持、土地保护等法律法规的要求，突出“以人为本、服务运输、系统优化、着眼发展”的设计理念，依据铁路网规划、城市总体规划和综合交通规划，系统分析客货运输要求，统筹协调车站及枢纽设施设备的布局，选择适宜的标准，合理确定车站及枢纽设计方案。

铁路车站及枢纽设计须符合《铁路车站及枢纽设计规范》（TB 10099—2017）的规定。

4. Design Requirements and Technical Standards of Railway Station and Terminal

The design of railway station and terminal shall fully implement the requirements of laws and regulations, e.g. ecological environment protection, soil and water conservation, land protection, etc., highlight the design concept of "people-oriented, serve for transportation, system optimization, development-oriented". Systematically analyze requirements of passenger and freight transportation according to railway network planning, overall city planning and comprehensive transportation planning. Coordinate the layout of station and setting of terminal facilities and equipment. Select appropriate standards to determine reasonable design schemes of station and terminal.

The design of railway station and terminal shall comply with the provisions of "Code for Design of Railway Station and Terminal" （TB 10099-2017）.

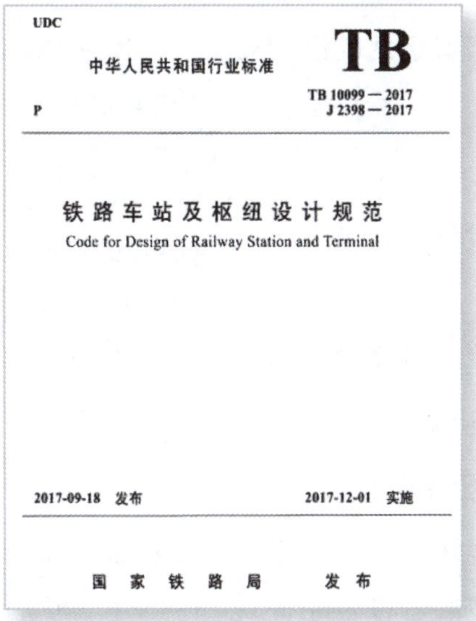

图 7-23　行业标准《铁路车站及枢纽设计规范》（TB 10099—2017）

Figure 7-23　Industry Standard Code for "Design of Railway Station and Terminal"（TB 10099-2017）

5. 做好高速铁路环境影响评价

减少高速铁路噪声、振动、污水与固体废弃物、废气、电磁辐射、微气压波等对城市环境的影响。

5. Make a Good Assessment of Environmental Impact of High Speed Railway

Reduce the impact of noise, vibration, sewage and solid wastes, waste gas, electromagnetic radiation, micro-pressure waves, etc. on urban environment.

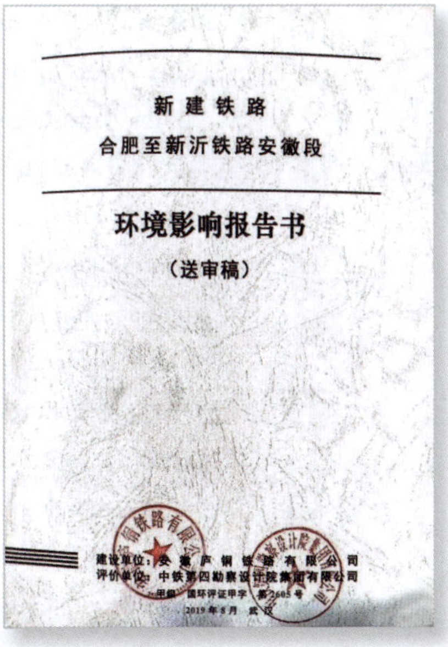

图 7-24　新建铁路合肥至新沂铁路安徽段环境影响报告书

Figure 7-24　Environmental Impact Report for Anhui Section of Newly-Built Hefei-Xinyi Railway Line

知识点二：高速铁路客运站的设计原则

高速铁路客运站的设计应遵循下列原则：

（1）引入铁路枢纽应与城市总体规划及铁路枢纽总图规划相协调。

（2）铁路枢纽内客运站的数量应根据枢纽客运布局、枢纽客运量、引入线路数量、客车开行方案及既有设备配置等因素综合确定。

（3）铁路枢纽内有两个及以上客运站时，客运站的分工应根据客车径路顺畅、点线能力协调、旅客乘降方便等原则，按引入方向、客车类别、客车开行方案等方式确定。

（4）客运站选址应满足运输需求并与城市规划相协调，考虑地形地质条件、既有建筑物拆迁、土地资源开发和城市发展等因素，经综合比选后确定。

（5）客运站应考虑与城市交通系统相协调，方便旅客换乘。

Key Point 2: Design Principles of High Speed Railway Passenger Station

The design of high speed railway passenger station shall comply with the following principles:

(1) Introducing railway terminal shall be coordinated with city overall planning and railway terminal overall planning.

(2) The number of passenger stations in a railway terminal shall be comprehensively determined by factors such as terminal passenger transport layout, terminal passenger capacity, number of lead-in lines, passenger train operation plan, and existing equipment, etc.

(3) When there are two or more passenger stations in a railway terminal, the division of labor among passenger stations shall be determined by principles of smooth passenger train route, coordination ability of points and lines, convenience of passengers on and off, etc. It is also determined by introduction direction, type of passenger trains, passenger train operation plan, etc.

(4) The site selection of passenger station shall meet transportation needs and coordinate with city overall planning, taking into account terrain and geological condition, demolition of existing buildings, development of land resources, urban development and other factors, and comes into final decision after comprehensive comparison and selection.

(5) Passenger station should consider the coordination with urban transport system to facilitate passenger transfer.

学习笔记

Study Notes

模块三　课堂练习

2019年9月，为深入推进长江经济带发展，加快构建京昆高速铁路通道，加强成渝城市群和滇中城市群的联系，促进沿线经济、社会发展和脱贫攻坚，国家发展改革委批复同意新建重庆至昆明高速铁路。高铁线路自重庆西站引出，经重庆市江津区、永川区，四川省泸州市、宜宾市，贵州省毕节市，云南省昭通市、曲靖市，终至昆明南站。正线全长699千米，其中新建正线681千米，以及在建自贡至宜宾高速铁路18千米。全线设站20座（预留车站1座）。

问题1：请说明渝昆高铁云南段站点设置情况。

问题2：请以小组讨论的形式，从站点设置、线路走向等方面分析渝昆高铁对昆明铁路枢纽的影响。

问题3：请以小组讨论的形式，分析渝昆高铁对昆明长水国际机场的影响。

Module 3　In-class Exercises

In September 2019, to further promote the development of the Yangtze River Economic Belt, speed up the construction of Beijing-Kunming High Speed Railway, strengthen the links between Chengdu-Chongqing urban agglomeration and central Yunnan urban agglomeration, promote economic and social development along the belt and alleviate poverty, the National Development and Reform Commission approved the construction of Chongqing-Kunming High Speed Railway. The high speed railway line leads from Chongqing West Railway Station to Kunming South Railway Station via Jiangjin District and Yongchuan District of Chongqing City, Luzhou City and Yibin City of Sichuan Province, Bijie City of Guizhou Province, Zhaotong City and Qujing City of Yunnan Province. The total length of main line is 699 km, of which 681km is newly-built main line and 18km is being-built Zigong-Yibin High Speed Railway. There are 20 stations along the whole line (one station is reserved).

Question 1: Make a discussion on station setting of Yunnan section of Chongqing-Kunming High Speed Railway.

Question 2: Make group discussions and analyze the impact of Chongqing-Kunming High Speed Railway on Kunming Railway Terminal from the perspective of station setting and route trend.

Question 3: Make group discussions and analyze the impact of Chongqing-Kunming High Speed Railway on Kunming Changshui International Airport.

课堂练习

In-class Exercises

模块四　课后拓展

分析云桂铁路的开通给沿线城市旅游发展带来的影响。

请选择云桂铁路云南段沿线任一开通高铁的县级城市，就出行时间，交通成本，交通便利性，旅游资源的特色化、专业化、差异化，生态环境保护等方面作出分析。

Module 4　After-class Activity

Analyzes the impact of opening Yunnan-Guangxi Railway on tourism development of cities along the line.

Please choose a county-level city with high speed train in Yunnan section of Yunnan-Guangxi Railway, and make analyses in terms of travel time, transportation cost, traffic convenience, specialization, profession and differentiation of tourism resources, and ecological environment protection, etc.

课后拓展

After-class Activity

任务三　高速铁路通过大城市铁路枢纽的技术方案

Task 3　Technical Scheme for High Speed Railway Passing through Railway Terminal in Metropolis

模块一　学前准备

查阅资料，在云南已开通高铁和动车组的车站中，列出所有与既有站合设或由既有站改造的车站，并列出途经线路。

Module 1　Preparation before Class

Do research on stations with high speed trains and Electric Multiple Units in Yunnan Province, list all combined or renovated existing stations, as well as their passing routes.

课前学习笔记

Study Notes before Class

模块二　课堂学习

知识点一：高速铁路通过大城市铁路枢纽的技术方案

高速铁路通过大城市铁路枢纽时，根据高铁车站设置和高速铁路线路走向，可归纳为三种基本技术方案：

（1）利用既有站、调整既有站分工或利用既有站改建高速铁路车站。

高速铁路正线利用既有线引入车站或高速铁路正线直接接入车站。

高速铁路正线多为靠近既有线穿越市区走行。这种站、线的组合，在高速铁路通过大城市枢纽中受到较广泛的应用。

（2）在既有车站附近建高铁车站，依托既有客站站房等设施作为高速铁路客运设施，高铁车站与既有站不直接连通，高速铁路线路引入新建的高铁车站。

（3）在现有市区以外，与城市规划发展相应的位置新建高铁车站。

Module 2　In-class Learning

Key Point 1：Technical Scheme for High Speed Railway Passing through Railway Terminal in Metropolis

When high speed railways pass through railway terminals in metropolis，the technical scheme includes three basic types according to the arrangement of high speed railway station and the trend of high speed railway line：

（1）High speed station built by using existing station，adjusting division of labor of existing station or reconstructing existing station. The main line of high speed railway is introduced into station by existing line or directly connected to station. Most main lines of high speed railway run close to the existing line and pass through urban areas. This combination of station and line is widely used in high speed railway passing through railway terminal in metropolis.

（2）Build a high speed railway station near the existing station. By using existing facilities，e.g. existing passenger station building，as high speed passenger transport facilities. High speed railway station is not directly connected with the existing station. High speed railway lines are introduced into the newly-built high speed railway station.

（3）In addition to the existing urban areas，new high speed railway station will be built at locations corresponding to city overall planning and development.

知识点二：高速铁路车站与既有站合设

Key Point 2：Combine High Speed Railway Station with Existing Station

图 7–25　广州南站

Figure 7–25　Guangzhou South Railway Station

1. 高速铁路车站与既有站合设的优点

（1）有利于吸引客流。既有客运站一般位于城市中心附近，高速铁路车站与其合并设置，便于旅客乘降，节省出行时间。

（2）可充分利用既有客运站的站场、站房及其他旅客服务设施，节省工程投资和城市用地。

（3）有利于旅客换乘。高速铁路、跨线列车的旅客可在同一车站直接换乘，无须乘坐市内交通工具，不仅可以减轻城市交通负担，也可以节省旅客换乘时间。

1. Advantages of Combining High Speed Railway Station with Existing Station

（1）Attract passenger flow. Existing passenger stations are generally located near city center. Combine high speed railway station with existing station to facilitate passengers on and off and save travel time.

（2）Save project investment and urban land–use by making full use of existing passenger station and yard，station building and other passenger service facilities.

（3）Convenient for passenger transfer. Passengers of high speed and cross–line trains can directly transfer at the same station without taking city traffic，which can not only reduce traffic in city，but also save passengers transfer time.

2. 高速铁路车站与既有站合设的设计原则

（1）由于高速铁路线路上列车运行采用自动控制和调度集中，高速列车的运行及其接发进路应单独自成系统，普速列车不得进入高速系统。但跨线列车的接发既需在高速系统进行，又需在普速系统进行。因此，在高、普速列车共站的车站上，为便于运营管理，高、普速列车宜分场分线使用。

（2）在跨线列车需上、下高速线运行的车站，高速列车车场与普速列车车场之间应利用渡线或具有立交疏解设备的联络线互相连通，以保证转场作业的顺利进行和列车接发的机动性。在没有跨线列车上、下高速线的车站，因两场无须连通，也可不设这种联络线或渡线。

（3）客运站房共用。为了便于旅客换乘，确保高速旅客流线与普速旅客流线互不交叉，高速铁路旅客与普速铁路旅客的进、出站通路及其候车室应尽量分开。

2. Design Principles of Combining High Speed Railway Station with Existing Station

（1）Automatic control and centralized dispatching are adopted for high speed train operation，so the high speed train operation and its receiving–departure routes shall be a separate system. Normal speed trains shall not enter into the high speed system. However, the arrival and departure of cross–line trains need to be carried out both in high speed system and normal speed system. Therefore, in a station with both high speed and normal speed trains，the two kinds of trains should be put into different yards and lines for operation and management convenience.

（2）In station where cross–line trains need to run on and off high speed line，the high speed and normal speed yards should be connected with each other by crossovers or connecting lines with vertical untwining equipment，so as to ensure smooth transition operation and mobility of train arrival–departure. In station without cross–line trains to run on and off high speed line，the high speed yard and normal speed yard do not connect. There is no need to set the connecting line or crossover.

（3）Shared passenger station building. To facilitate passenger transfer and ensure that high speed passenger flow line does not cross over normal speed passenger flow line， the entrance/exit access road and waiting room for high speed and normal speed railway passengers shall be separated as far as possible.

3. 高速铁路车站与既有站合设的布置方式

高速铁路车站与既有站合设时，究竟采用何种布置方案，应根据城市规划、既有客运站设备、当地地形地物、高速铁路线路引入枢纽的方式以及工程投资、施工难易程度等因素，通过技术、经济比选后确定。

（1）高速列车与普速列车共用车场。

高速铁路正线不直接引入既有站。高速铁路正线在枢纽前方站与既有线正线连接。利用既有线正线进入枢纽，利用既有线正线进入既有客运站。既有客运车场为高速列车与普速列车共用股道，如上海站。

优点：节省高速铁路线路引入枢纽的建筑费用。

缺点：作业交叉干扰大，指挥和组织复杂。

3. Arrangement of Combining High Speed Railway Station with Existing Station

When high speed station is combined with existing station, the layout scheme shall be determined by technical and economical comparison and selection based on factors such as city overall planning, existing passenger station equipment, local terrain condition, the way high speed line is introduced into terminal, project investment, and degree of construction difficulty, etc.

(1) Shared yard for high speed and normal speed trains.

High speed main line is not directly introduced to existing station. High speed main line is connected with existing main line at the station in advance of terminal. To enter terminal or passenger station by existing main line. The existing passenger yard has common tracks for high speed and normal speed trains, e.g. Shanghai Railway Station.

Advantages: saving construction cost of introducing high speed line into terminal.

Disadvantages: large cross-interference in operation and complicated control and organization.

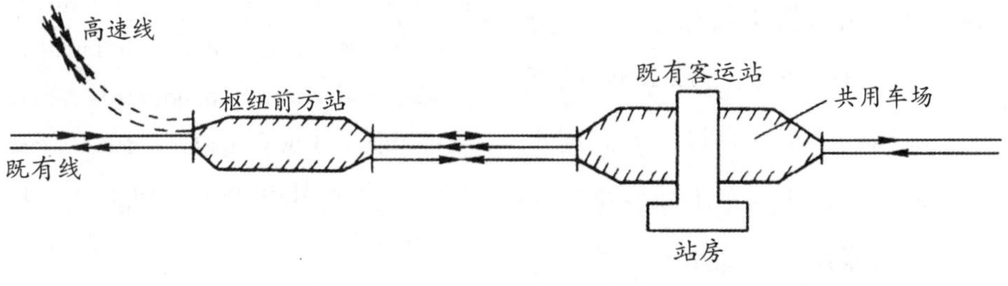

高速线 high speed line　既有线 existing line　枢纽前方站 station in advance of terminal

既有客运站 existing passenger station　站房 station building　共用车场 shared yard

图 7-26　高速列车与普速列车共用车场布置示意图

Figure 7-26　Schematic Figure of Shared Yard Arrangement for High Speed and Normal Speed Train

上海站为京沪铁路、沪昆铁路、沪宁城际铁路途经站。其站台为岛式和侧式混合站台，共设有7个站台，包括1个侧式站台和6个岛式站台；共13个站台面，14股道，包括12条到发线和2条机走线。

Beijing-Shanghai Railway, Shanghai-Kunming Railway and Shanghai-Nanjing Intercity Railway are all passing through Shanghai Railway Station. Its platform is a mixed island/side platform with 7 platforms, including 1 side platform, 6 island platforms, 13 platform surfaces and 14 tracks, of which are 13 arrival-departure tracks and 2 locomotive running tracks in the station.

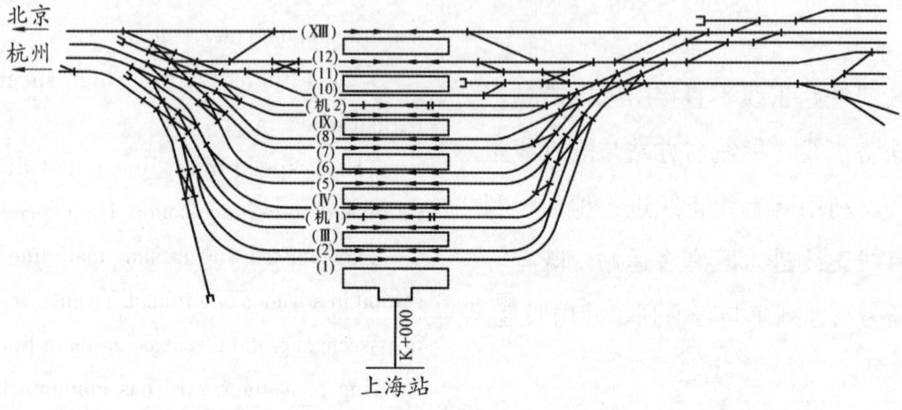

上海站 Shanghai Railway Station　北京 Beijing　杭州 Hangzhou　机 locomotive running track

图 7-27　上海站站台布局示意图

Figure 7-27　Schematic Figure of Platform Setting in Shanghai Railway Station

（2）高速车场与普速车场咽喉互不连通。

高速铁路引入枢纽既有客运站，分别设置高速、普速车场，两车场咽喉互不连通。高速铁路正线直接引入高速车场。高速列车与普速列车不能直接进入对方车场。高速列车与普速列车的运行成为互不干扰、互相独立的两个系统。

适用：跨线旅客列车不上、下高速线的车站。

（2）No connection between throats of high speed and normal speed yard.

Introducing high speed railway into existing passenger station in terminal with high speed and normal speed yards respectively. The throat of two yards are not connected with each other. Main line of high speed railway is directly introduced into high speed yard. High speed train and normal speed train cannot directly enter into each other's yard. Operations of high speed train and normal speed train are two independent systems that do

优点：作业无交叉，干扰不大，指挥和组织简单。

缺点：跨线列车不能上、下高速线。

not interfere with each other.

Applicable for: stations where cross-line passenger trains do not run on and off high speed line.

Advantages: no cross-interference, simple control and organization.

Disadvantages: cross-line trains cannot run on or off high speed line.

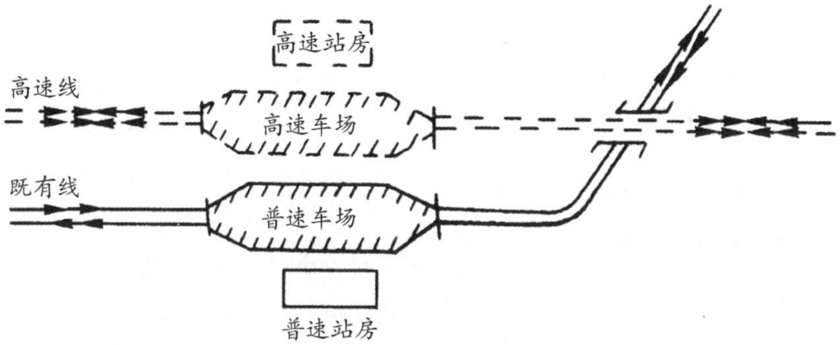

高速线 high speed line　高速站房 high speed station building　高速车场 high speed yard
普速车场 normal speed yard　既有线 existing line　普速站房 normal speed station building

图 7-28　高速车场与普速车场咽喉互不连通布置示意图

Figure 7-28　Schematic Figure of Throat Arrangement Unconnected between High Speed and Normal Speed Yard

（3）高速车场与普速车场在同一平面并列合设。

图 7-29（a）为高速线与既有线并行引入既有尽端式客运站布置图。将靠近既有主站房一侧的既有到发线和站台改建为高速车场，供接发高速列车之用；与高速车场并列的其他到发线和站台作为普速车场，且在外侧适当扩建，供接发普速列车之用。在既有站房对侧，新建副站房，主站房与副站房之间采用高架通廊和地道相连，供旅客进、出站和换乘。两车场的进口咽喉用渡线互相连

（3）Parallel arrangement of high speed and normal speed yards on the same plane.

Figure 7-29（a）is a layout of introducing high speed line and existing line into existing dead-end passenger station in parallel. Reconstructing existing arrival-departure line and platform near one side of existing main station building into a high speed yard for high speed train receiving-departure. Other receiving-departure lines and platforms parallel to high speed yard will be used as normal speed yard. It can be appropriately expanded on the outside for normal speed train receiving-departure. On the opposite

通。高速列车的动车段以及既有普速列车的客车整备场和机务段都有单独的站段联络线相衔接，以保证咽喉区必需的平行进路。

适用：以办理始发、终到高速列车业务为主的高速铁路车站。

图 7–29（b）为高速线与既有线并行引入既有通过式客运站的布置图。既有线在站房一侧，高速线在站房对侧。高速车场与普速车场横列，两车场咽喉用渡线互相连通。高速车场向外适当扩建。为便于高速旅客列车的旅客出入站，采用高架通廊和地道相连。

适用：以通过高速列车为主的车站。

缺点：由于两车场横列布置，两端咽喉区高速、跨线列车到发进路交叉较严重。

side of existing station building, build a new auxiliary station building. Main station building and auxiliary station building are connected by elevated corridor and underpass tunnel for passengers to enter, exit and transfer. Entrance throats of two yards are connected by crossovers. EMU depot of high speed train, passenger car servicing yard and locomotive depot of existing normal speed train have separate connecting lines to ensure the necessary parallel route in throat area.

Applicable for: handling high speed station with arrival–departure high speed trains.

Figure 7–29 (b) is a layout for parallel introduction of high speed line and existing line into existing through–type passenger station. The existing line is on one side of station building and the high speed line is on the opposite side of station building. High speed yard and normal speed yard are arranged horizontally, throats of two yards are connected by crossovers, and high speed yard is appropriately expanded outward. Elevated corridor and underpass tunnel are adopted to facilitate high speed train passenger entry and exit.

Applicable for: station mainly with high speed train passing.

Disadvantages: Due to the horizontal arrangement of two yards, there are serious crossing problems in receiving–departure tracks at throat areas at both ends for high speed and cross–line trains.

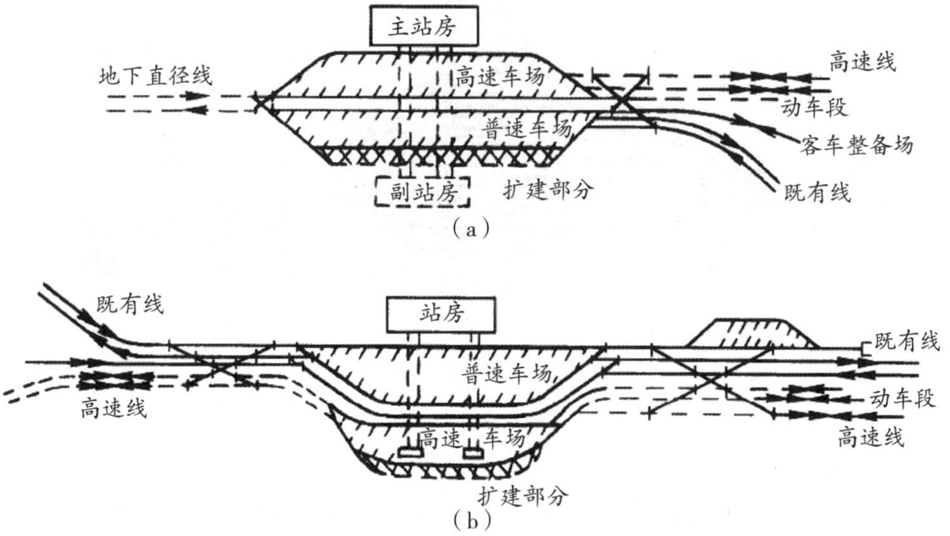

地下直径线 underground diameter line　主站房 main station building　副站房 auxiliary station building
高速车场 high speed yard　普速车场 normal speed yard　扩建部分 expansion part
高速线 high speed line　动车段 EMU depot　客车整备场 passenger car servicing yard
既有线 existing line　站房 station building

图 7–29　高速车场与普速车场在同一平面并列合设布置示意图

Figure 7–29　Schematic Figure of Parallel Arrangement of High Speed and Normal Speed Yard on the Same Plane

北京站是京沪铁路、京哈铁路、京承铁路、丰沙铁路、京原铁路、京广铁路、京九铁路等多条客运专线及城际高速铁路的交会节点；开往东北方向、华东地区的列车及出境列车（K3/K4 次列车、K19/K20 次列车、K27/K28 次列车）等在该站始发。

北京站设 16 条股道和 8 座站台。其中包括 1 座侧式站台和 5 座岛式站台，编号 1~14。站台和站房间有 2 座天桥、2 条地下通道和中央检票通廊连接。

Beijing Railway Station is the meeting point of many passenger dedicated lines and intercity high speed railways, e.g. Beijing–Shanghai Railway, Beijing–Harbin Railway, Beijing–Chengde Railway, Fengtai–Shacheng Railway, Beijing–Yuanping Railway, Beijing–Guangzhou Railway and Beijing–Kowloon Railway. Trains to the northeast, Eastern China and outbound（Train K3/K4, Train K19/K20, Train K27/K28）departure at this station.

Beijing Railway Station has 16 tracks and 8 platforms, which includes one side platform and five island platforms, numbered 1~14. Platform and station building are connected by two overpasses, two underpass tunnels and a central ticket check–in corridor.

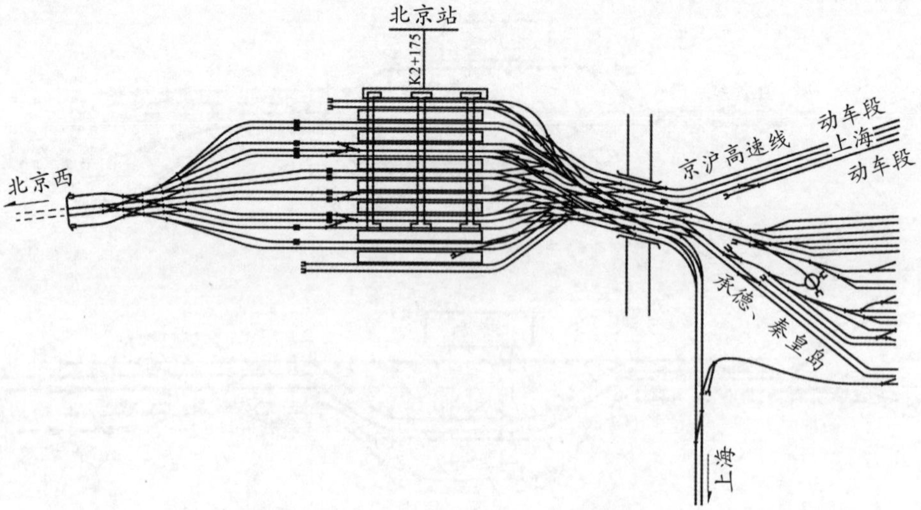

北京站 Beijing Railway Station　北京西 Beijing West

京沪高速线 Beijing-Shanghai High Speed Railway Line　动车段 EMU depot　上海 Shanghai

承德 Chengde　秦皇岛 Qinhuangdao

图 7-30　北京站站台线路布局示意图

Figure 7-30　Schematic Figure of Layout of Platform Line in Beijing Railway Station

（4）既有站上方设高架高速车场。

高速线高架引入既有站，在既有站上方设高架高速车场，承担接发高速旅客列车和通过车站不停车的跨线旅客列车的任务。桥下地面既有站为普速车场，承担接发始发、终到停站通过的普速旅客列车的任务。

两车场两端采用进站线路立交疏解设备互相连通，便于跨线客车上、下高速线。但当没有跨线列车上、下高速线时，两车场之间也可不必连通，以节省工程费用。

高速旅客列车的旅客可通过主、副站房的自动扶梯和高架候车室通廊而进、出站和换乘。普速旅客列车的旅客可通过高架候车室和地道进、出站。

（4）Setting elevated high speed yard above existing station.

Elevated high speed lines are introduced into existing station. Elevated high speed yard is set up above existing station to undertake high speed passenger trains receiving and departure and cross-line passenger train passing through station without stopping. Existing ground station under bridge is set up as normal speed yard which is responsible for normal speed passenger trains receiving and departure.

The two ends of two yards are connected by using station approach track and vertical untwining equipment，so as to facilitate cross-line train to run on and off high speed line. However，if no cross-line trains running on and off high speed line，there is no need to connect two yards，so as to save project cost.

High speed railway passengers can

enter, exit and transfer by escalators in main and auxiliary station buildings and elevated waiting room corridor.While normal speed railway passengers can enter and exit station by elevated waiting room and underpass tunnel.

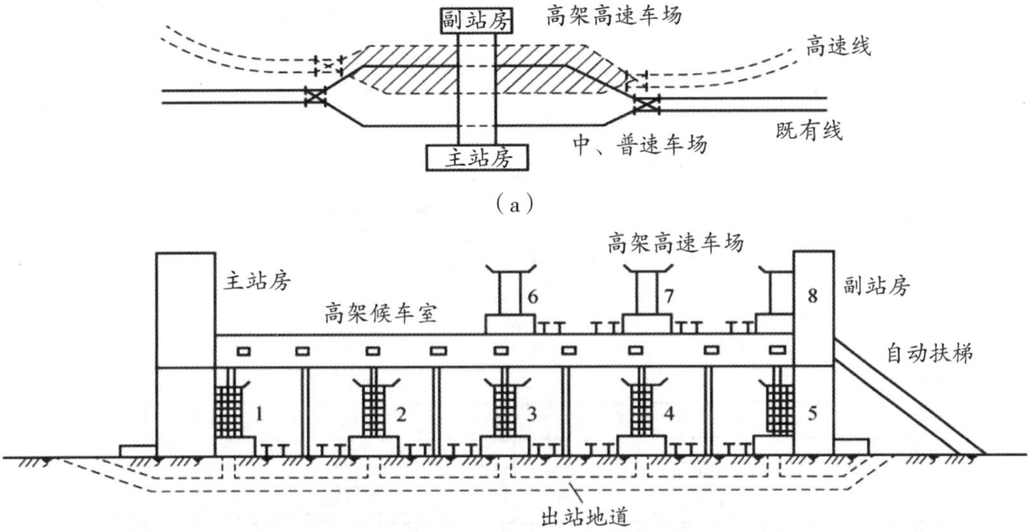

(a)　(b)

主站房 main station building　副站房 auxiliary station building　高架高速车场 elevated high speed yard
中、普速车场 medium and normal speed yard　高速线 high speed line　既有线 existing line
高架候车室 elevated waiting room　自动扶梯 escalator　出站地道 exit underpass tunnel

图 7-31　既有站上方设高架高速车场布置示意图

Figure 7-31　Schematic Figure of Setting Elevated High Speed Yard above Existing Station

说明：1~5 为中、普速车场站台，6~8 为高速车场站台。

Note: 1~5 platforms are platforms of medium and normal speed yard, 6~8 platforms are platforms of high speed yard.

（5）既有站下方设地下高速车场。

高速线从地下引入既有站，在既有站地下新建高速车场。将既有站改建为普速车场，其车场的固定用途与图 7-32 相同。两车场两端采用进站线路疏解设备相连接，以便跨线列车上、下高速线。高速旅客列车的旅客可沿地道和自动扶

(5) Setting underground high speed yard under existing station.

High speed lines are introduced into existing station from underground, building a new high speed yard under existing station. Existing station is reconstructed into a normal speed yard, its fixed usage is the same as that shown in Figure 7-32 above. The two

梯进、出站和换乘。普速旅客列车的旅客可沿高架候车室和地道进、出站。

ends of the two yards are connected by station approach track untwining equipment, so as to facilitate cross-line trains to run on and off high speed line. High speed railway passengers can enter, exit and transfer by underpass tunnel and escalator. While normal speed railway passengers can enter and exit station along elevated waiting room and underpass tunnel.

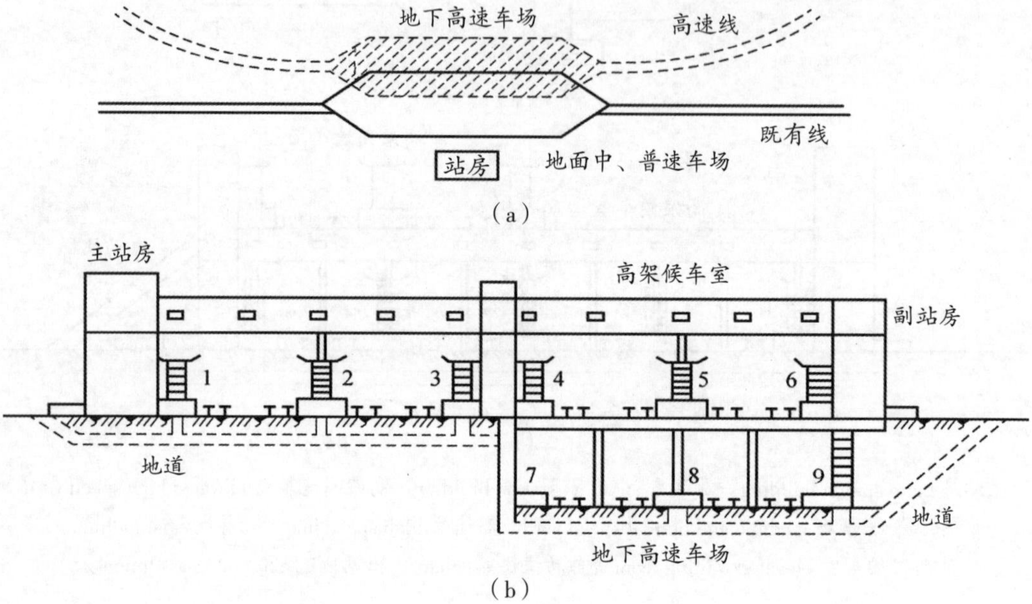

地下高速车场 underground high speed yard　站房 station building
地面中、普速车场 medium and normal speed ground yard　高速线 high speed line　既有线 existing line
主站房 main station building　副站房 auxiliary station building　高架候车室 elevated waiting room
地下高速车场 underground high speed yard　地道 underpass tunnel

图 7–32　既有站下方设地下高速车场布置示意图

Figure 7–32　Schematic Figure of Layout of Setting Underground High Speed Yard under Existing Station

说明：1~6 为中、普速车场站台，7~9 为高速车场站台。

Note: 1~6 platforms are platforms of medium and normal speed yard, 7~9 platforms are platforms of high speed yard.

高速线地下设站形式由于其工程造价高，施工困难，因而非特殊困难情况，很少采用。

Due to high construction cost and difficulties, setting underground station for high speed line is seldom adopted except for special difficult cases.

学习笔记

Study Notes

模块三　课堂练习

问题 1：做小组讨论，列举 5 个利用既有站的铁路车站，并说明这 5 个车站符合高速铁路车站与既有站合设的哪种布置方式。

问题 2：简述昆明南站在昆明铁路枢纽中的地位、功能及作用。

Module 3　In-class Exercises

Question 1：Make group discussion and list five railway stations using existing station. Explain the layout of five stations which are combined by high speed railway station and existing station.

Question 2：Briefly describe the status, function and use of Kunming South Railway Station in Kunming Railway Terminal.

课堂练习

In-class Exercises

模块四　课后拓展

简述中泰铁路中国段和泰国段车站设置及建设情况。

Module 4　After-class Activity

Briefly describe the station setting and construction status of China section and Thailand section of China-Thailand Railway.

课后拓展

After-class Activity

参考文献

Reference

［1］陈应先 . 高速铁路线路与车站设计 . 北京：中国铁道出版社，2001.

［2］徐友良 . 高速铁路车站与线路 . 北京：中国铁道出版社，2012.

［3］刘向云，左锋等 . 高速铁路设计规范（试行）. 北京：中国铁道出版社，2010.

［4］中国铁路总公司 . 铁路技术管理规程 . 北京：中国铁道出版社，2014.

［5］王秋平 . 铁路线路与站场 . 西安：西安交通大学出版社，2020.

［6］中国国家铁路局 . 铁路线路设计规范 . 北京 : 中国铁道出版社，2017.

［7］中国国家铁路局 . 铁路车站及枢纽设计规范 . 北京 : 中国铁道出版社，2017.

［1］Chen Yingxian. Design of High Speed Railway Lines and Stations. Beijing: China Railway Publishing House, 2001.

［2］Xu Youliang. Stations and Lines of High Speed Railway. Beijing: China Railway Publishing House, 2012.

［3］Liu Xiangyun, Zuo Feng et al. Code for Design of High Speed Railway（Trial）. Beijing: China Railway Publishing House, 2010.

［4］China National Railway Group Limited. Railway Technical Management Regulations. Beijing：China Railway Publishing House, 2014.

［5］Wang Qiuping. Railway Lines and Stations. Xi' an: Xi' an Jiaotong University Press, 2020.

［6］National Railway Administration of the People' s Republic of China. Code for Design of Railway Lines. Beijing：China Railway Publishing House, 2017.

［7］National Railway Administration of the People' s Republic of China. Code for Design of Railway Stations and Hub. Beijing：China Railway Publishing House, 2017.